FAMILY SURVIVAL GUIDE

KAREN DOCKREY

VICTOR BOOKS ®

A DIVISION OF SCRIPTURE PRESS PUBLICATIONS INC.
USA CANADA ENGLAND

Second printing, 1988

All Bible quotations, unless otherwise indicated, are from the *Holy Bible, New International Version,* © 1973, 1978, 1984, International Bible Society. Used by permission of Zondervan Bible Publishers; other quotations are from the *Authorized (King James) Version* (KJV).

ISBN: 0-89693-458-6

CONTENTS

FAMILY SURVIVAL GUIDE is designed to help your young teens understand and take steps toward solving their family struggles. They'll learn not only how to survive but how to enjoy life with their families. As part of the Young Teen Feedback Elective series, this book presents creative Bible studies that will keep your young teens interested and challenge them to grow spiritually.

HOW TO USE YOUNG TEEN FEEDBACK ELECTIVES

You'll discover that these studies are especially geared toward young teens—a group in the midst of change. As they struggle to make the transition from children to adults, young teens show extremes of behavior—energetic one minute, withdrawn the next. These fast-paced studies offer a variety of teaching methods to appeal to these sometimes hard-to-interest group members. Each creative session is firmly founded on the Word of God.

Each lesson focuses on one or more Bible truths that can be applied directly to young teens' lives. Make sure you have enough Bibles so that students who forget theirs can borrow them. Try to have some modern-language translations on hand for easy comprehension.

If you're unfamiliar with Young Teen Feedback Electives, take a few minutes to study this overview of your elective study.

Flexible Format
Notice that you can study the topic of this book over a 12-week quarter. In addition, each subtopic is complete in itself, so you can study part of this elective for four weeks, returning to the other studies at a later time. This format gives you flexibility to suit your program to the particular needs of your young people. It also lets you tailor the study to your schedule.

Introductory Page
Each session has an easy-to-use summary of the lesson on the first page to help you see the lesson at a glance.

■ *Key Concept* clearly states the lesson's theme.
■ *Meeting the Need* outlines general concerns and questions young teens have on the session's subject. By understanding their concerns, you can better help teens apply the lesson.
■ *Session Goals* includes the objectives of the lesson in measurable terms. Each goal helps communicate the Key Concept and should be achieved by group members by the end of the session.
■ *Special Preparation* gives you a checklist of what you'll need to lead the session.

Building the Body
The first minutes of each session are devoted to relationship building. These exercises, activities, and optional "warm-ups" will help your group get to know one another and you—a key to an open group where good Bible study can take place. These activities also provide a transition

time which takes young teens away from outside concerns and points them toward the group study.

Launching the Lesson
This section offers focus discussions and activities that zero in on needs and interests that will be covered by the Bible study later in the lesson.

Exploring the Word
This part of the study contains creative ways to communicate Bible truths and concepts. It not only helps *you* share God's Word, but it also allows young teens to discover God's Word for themselves.

Applying the Truth
This application section summarizes Bible truths and concepts. It helps young teens relate Christian faith and values to their everyday lives, answering the question, "What does this mean to me?"

Workout Sheets
These activity sheets encourage young teens to discover concepts, facts, and ideas in a variety of ways. The sheets are meant to be reproduced. Just tear out the master copy and make as many duplicates as you need. You may want to provide folders for group members to collect and save their Workout Sheets.

Student Books
Student books are available to help bring home Bible truths to young teens in your group. These lively books are written by men and women who know how to communicate to your young people. They can be used many different ways:

■ Have group members read the chapter *after* each session so material covered in class will be reinforced and "come alive" at home.

■ Have group members read a chapter *before* each session to stimulate their thinking on the subject and get them ready for in-class discussions.

■ Use portions of the books *during* the group study. For instance, incorporate a case study from the book into a group discussion.

You can complete this elective study without using the student books, but we recommend them as an excellent tool to give students their own version of the material you study together. It's something permanent that they can refer to long after the group study has ended. These books are entertaining, informative, and fun to use. Their small size makes them portable; they fit easily into pockets or purses. Look for them at your local Christian bookstore, and add them to this elective study.

Before Each Lesson
Pray for your young teens as they work through this study. Ask the Lord to help you create an open atmosphere in your group, so that teens will feel free to share with each other and you.

After Each Lesson
Evaluate each session as you ask yourself the following questions: Did each student achieve the lesson goals? Why or why not? Did you have the right amount of time to complete the lesson? How many group members actively took part in the session? Are interpersonal relationships being nurtured in the group? How well did you prepare the lesson? How might you change your presentation next time?

PARENT PRESSURE

PART ONE

The advent of adolescence launches the journey toward a new type of relationship with parents. This journey is seldom an easy one for teenagers or their parents. Adolescents' increasing need for independence seems to clash with parents' need to continue directing. This unit attempts to guide young people toward understanding and blending both their needs and their parents' needs. The sessions are built on the premise that family peace is possible when both teenagers and their parents work toward it. It admits that conflict between teenagers and their parents is inevitable, so rather than feeling guilty about problems, families can commit their energies toward solving them.

These studies emphasize involvement learning. Rather than simply hearing about how to solve conflicts with their parents, your students will practice these skills. They'll discover for themselves how and why the Bible's relationship principles work. As you teach, resist the urge to sit your group down and tell them what every passage means. Bible truth impacts young people more deeply when they discover that truth for themselves. Guide them to interact with God's Word and with each other to discover His truth.

Several of the sessions suggest more activities than you may have time to do. This allows you to choose what works best for your group, and gives you backup material in case you have extra time.

Because of the sensitivity of these subjects, you may want to divide large groups into smaller discussion units when asking questions and sharing discoveries. Enlist a mature student or another adult to lead each smaller group.

Throughout all sessions assure your young teens that you realize that some live with one parent, others live with both parents, some live with one or more stepparents, and a few live with grandparents, an aunt, or a guardian. Explain that in these sessions, you mean all these when you say "parent."

PARENT PRESSURE

WHY THE PROBLEMS? (Romans 12:9-18; 14:19)

KEY CONCEPT

Conflicts with parents intensify as young people enter the teen years and begin their journey toward independence.

MEETING THE NEED

This session will respond to the following student questions and comments:
- "My parents don't love me anymore."
- "Why can't I get along with my parents?"
- "Don't my parents see that I'm no longer a child?"

SESSION GOALS

You will help each group member
1. list the problems he has with his parents,
2. suggest reasons for those problems,
3. pinpoint some actions that lead to solutions.

SPECIAL PREPARATION

____ Bring extra Bibles, 3″ x 5″ cards, markers, masking tape, paper, pencils, and chalk.
____ Bring a can or box and slips of paper (at least three per student) for "Canned Questions."
____ Gather problems or write sample list for "Here's What the Parents Say."
____ Bring the student books if you have them.
____ Write Romans 14:19 on cue cards for "Peace at Home."
____ Duplicate Workout Sheets #1 and #2.
____ Gather letters for "What Parents Wish Their Teenagers Knew."
____ Write "Response Letter" topics on the chalkboard.

BUILDING THE BODY

✓ CANNED QUESTIONS

Give each student three slips of paper and a pencil as he or she enters. Point out the large poster on which you've written these instructions: **Write three questions you have about your relationship with your parent(s).** Gather the questions in a can as students write them.

When most have finished, draw a few questions from the can and invite the group to answer the questions as well as they can. Explain: **Hearing each other's questions helps us know we share similar concerns. It also helps us focus on what we most want to know. Over the next four weeks, we'll address most of your questions. You may live with one parent, both parents, a stepparent, or a grandparent. In these sessions, I mean all these when I say "parent." You'll have struggles with whoever is the parent in your home. But there are answers to those struggles. The answers come from God. Keep asking until you discover and understand God's answers.**

Return all questions to the can to deal with more fully in the next three sessions.

✓ PLUS AND MINUS

Sit in a large circle, and allow group members to share the best things that happened between them and their parents today and the worst things that happened. If they have not seen their parents today, suggest that they tell about the last time they were together.

Point out: **Any time we talk about parents, it's easy to get into a gripe session. And though griping can help, we don't want to stay there. Most relationships with parents have positive points as well as negative. Focusing on the positive can help us improve the negatives. In these sessions we hope to acquire skills that can help us build or rebuild strong relationships with our parents.**

LAUNCHING THE LESSON

✓ PARENT PROBLEM CHAINS

Divide into groups of about six. Give each group a stack of 3" x 5" cards and a marker. Challenge each group to make the longest chain of parent problems. Each problem must begin with the last letter of the previous problem. (Examples: Naggin**g**—**G**etting enough mone**y**—**Y**ou don't trust m**e**—**E**xcess rules. . . . Suggest that one person write and another tape the cards together into a long chain.

Call for two representatives from each group to hold and compare the length of their chain with the chains of the other groups. Congratulate the group with the longest chain. Tape all the chains to the wall, and refer to them for problem ideas throughout this unit.

AND HERE'S WHAT THE PARENTS SAY

Read and display a list of problems that you have gathered from parents of teenagers prior to this session. (To gather the problems from parents, ask the members of an adult Sunday School class to jot down a list of the five greatest problems between parents and teenagers.) If you don't have the opportunity to talk with parents, use this list gathered from church parents:

- It's hard to agree on acceptable entertainment (movies, television, books, etc.).
- Teenagers feel parents don't understand.
- Young people don't want parents to point out the dangers of foolish behavior.
- Teenagers feel we don't trust them.
- Lack of communication.
- Teenagers won't pick up after themselves.
- Teenagers have a know-it-all attitude.
- Young people often don't seem to see the consequences of their actions.
- Neither parents nor teens are willing to compromise.
- Money—teenagers don't seem to know there's an end.
- Drugs and alcohol.
- Clothes—what to choose and how much to spend.
- Getting along with brothers and sisters.

Ask: **How are our lists and the parents' lists similar? Where are the differences?** Point out: **At least we agree on what many of the problems are! Finding areas of agreement is one of the first steps to solving relationship problems.**

STUDENT BOOK OPTION

Direct students to find a problem in the "From Teenager's Viewpoint" list that matches one in the "From Parent's Viewpoint" list. Ask: **How might a teenager and parent work together to solve this problem?** Call for several to share their suggestions. (Example: "My parents ask too many questions" matches "My daughter never tells me anything." To work together, the teenager could tell the parent a couple things about an activity before she asks. The parent would then not have to ask so many questions.)

If you do not have the student books, complete the same exercise with the complaints from "Parent Problem Chains" and "And Here's What the Parents Say."

EXPLORING THE WORD

PEACE AT HOME

Write Romans 14:19, one word to a card, and display the cards in scrambled order. Have the group put them in order. (In the NIV: "Let us therefore make every effort to do what leads to peace and to mutual edification.") Invite students to read the verse from their own Bibles. Call on several to read the verse from different translations, if available. Point out that reading the verse in several Bible translations makes its meaning clearer. Ask: **What is peace?** (Example: Not just the absence of war but an inner feeling of calmness and security.) **What is edification?** (Examples: Encouraging one another to live God's way; building one another up.)

Guide the group to repeat the verse in unison, using the cards as cues. Remove two cards and repeat. Continue removing cards until the group recites the verse from memory.

Provide blank cards and direct students to write Romans 14:19 in the translation they like best and to decorate the card. Encourage them to keep it in their billfolds or purses or where they will see it daily. Point out: **This was Paul's advice for people in the thick of conflict. It can remind us of things we can do to promote family peace. We'll share some of the ways we've done this in a later session.** (Session 3)

PEACE-PROMOTING ACTIONS

Direct the students to open their Bibles to Romans 12:9-18. Call on a volunteer to read Romans 12:18. Explain: **This passage suggests several actions that can encourage peace with our parents. Find a partner or two and together find peace-promoting actions in verses 9-17. List them on paper and, beside each, name a way to do this in your family. For example: "Romans 12:9 encourages us to love sincerely. I can follow that in my family by not buttering up my dad just to get spending money."** Provide paper and markers and encourage your students as they work. OPTION: If your time is short, assign each pair one verse and give them a few minutes to find the action(s) and examples.

Call for teams to share their discoveries, one action and example at a time. Compliment the insight in each.

Ask: **How easy is it to do all these things at your house?** After several students have shared, agree that family peace is hard. Ask: **Why do you think problems between parents and children intensify when the teen years arrive?** Supplement their responses with: **You want more independence, and parents aren't used to giving it; parents did everything for you when you were a baby, and it's hard for many to let go; parents worry that something will happen to you; you have more choices to make.** If you have the student book, have your students search Laura's story in chapter 1 for more detailed reasons.

APPLYING THE TRUTH

Give at end of session

WORKOUT SHEET

Instruct your group members to write a wish list of everything they want from their parents, to fold it, and to give it to you. Explain that you'll give their unopened lists back in a few moments.

Give each student a copy of Workout Sheet #1 and challenge them to decode the wheel. (Solution: Parents are people like you.) Explain: **When we realize that our parents share many of the same feelings, worries, and interests that we have, we find it easier to solve our parent problems.** Under "Where do you see evidence . . ." students should list feelings, worries, and interests they and their parents have in common. (Examples: Worry what their peers think about them; become angry or frustrated; sometimes say things they don't mean; get depressed; love God; need to be loved.)

Call for students to take turns naming one thing they jotted down. Give back their wish lists and have them circle on their wish lists everything they think their parents also wish from them. (Examples: Understanding; don't expect perfection; show me you love me.)

√ WORKOUT SHEET

Distribute Workout Sheet #2. Explain that this letter is a combination of actual thoughts from actual parents. Instruct students to underline feelings they think their parents have, at least occasionally.

Discuss: **Why do you think this parent wrote a letter rather than saying these things? If your parents wrote you a letter, what do you think they would say to you?**

OPTION: Invite parents of your group members to write anonymous letters on the topic "What parents want their teenage children to know about them." Read these one at a time and discuss them as suggested above. If you have contact with all your students' parents, you might encourage them to write actual letters to their own teenagers. Do not distribute them in class unless you have a letter for *every* young person present.

√ RESPONSE LETTERS

Distribute stationery or plain paper. Encourage each student to write a letter to one or both parents on one or all of these topics which you have written on the chalkboard:
1 * ● What I want you to understand about me
2 * ● Why I love you
3 * ● What I want our relationship to be like

Insist that students refrain from criticizing their parents in the letters.

Instruct them to sit as far apart from one another as your room allows. This encourages privacy and cuts down on self-consciousness. Provide envelopes and instruct students to seal their letters in the envelopes when they finish. Encourage them to give the letters to their parents or to leave them where their parents will find them.

Close the letter experience with such questions as:
- **Why is it sometimes easier to write a letter than to talk about our feelings?** (Examples: Gives us time to calm down and sort things out; talking about deep feelings can be embarrassing.)
- **When does it cause more problems?** (Examples: Letter might be taken wrong and you wouldn't have opportunity to clear it up; might write negative feelings and feel different afterward.)

Suggest that when teenagers have difficulty talking with their parents they write letters. Emphasize: **Talking with each other about the letters after they are written and read can make them clearer and sort out any miscommunication.**

Encourage your group members: **Join us for the next three sessions as we detail three of the most important strategies for getting along with parents: communication, conflict solving, and trust building.**

SESSION 2

WORKING TOWARD CLEAR COMMUNICATION (James 3:2-10)

KEY CONCEPT

Clear communication can solve or prevent many problems teens have with their parents.

MEETING THE NEED

This session will respond to the following student questions and comments:
- "If my parents love me, why don't they show it?"
- "My parents just don't understand me."
- "Talking to my parents does absolutely no good."

SESSION GOALS

You will help each group member
1. identify four ways to communicate,
2. discover key biblical truths about communication,
3. practice clear communication strategies.

SPECIAL PREPARATION

____ Bring pencils, paper, markers, masking tape, and chalk.
____ Bring the question can begun last week.
____ Cut apart a copy of Workout Sheet #3 for each student.
____ Write the password cards.
____ Write COMMUNICATE vertically for "Imagine Great Communication."
____ Bring the student books if you have them.
____ Make a copy of Workout Sheet #4 and cut it apart. Place the situation cards in one sack and the reaction cards in another.

BUILDING THE BODY

BIRTHDAY JUMBLE

Arrange the chairs in one large circle. Explain the game: **When I call out two months, you who have birthdays in those months stand and find another seat. While you change seats, I will sit in one of the seats and leave one of you standing. You then call out two birthday months and find an empty seat during the jumble.** Begin and play for several minutes.

Explain: **We have just communicated. How?** Supplement student responses with: **Instead of asking each other when our birthdays are, we learned each other's birthday months by watching who stood during which months.** Select a few students and ask the group in which months these students were born. Point out: **There are many ways to communicate: We have just demonstrated communicating through** *actions.* **What are some others?** (Examples: Words; attitudes; tone of voice.) Emphasize: **Use all these methods to communicate with parents lovingly and clearly.**

CANNED QUESTIONS

Draw a few questions from the question can begun last week. Encourage the group to address them based on what you've studied so far. Supplement as needed. Return to the can any questions you haven't fully addressed. Encourage students to continue to add questions as they think of them.

LAUNCHING THE LESSON

WORKOUT SHEET

Point out: **We use communication to let other people know how we feel and what we need. As we learn how to communicate with our parents, we can strengthen our relationship with them. And good communication tends to be contagious!**

Duplicate a copy of Workout Sheet #3 for each student. Before class cut the four cards apart and shuffle them. Play a variation of the game Pit © by giving each player four cards and instructing them: **You have four cards which do not now match. Your goal is to get four matching cards by trading one at a time. When I say "GO," find someone who will trade one card without knowing what card you are trading. When you have four matching cards, shout the word on those cards and sit down.**

After all are seated, ask for four ways we communicate. (Actions, attitude, words, tone of voice.) Point out: **Because you were involved in trading, you memorized easily. Similarly, the more you are involved in communicating, the easier it becomes.**

HOW WE COMMUNICATE

Have the students quickly retrade their cards so they have one of all four methods. Direct them to hold up the card that answers each question:
- **How do you know when your parent is angry?**
- **How can you tell if it's a good time to ask your parents for something?**
- **How do you know if your parents understand what you are saying?**
- **How do you let your parents know you need their attention?**
- **How do you let your parents know you are upset?**
- **How do your parents show you they love you?**
- **How do you show your parents you care?**

Point out that noticing the ways we already communicate can help us pinpoint areas we want to improve and recognize the reasons we sometimes become frustrated in communication. Instruct students: **Write on the back of each of your four communication cards a way that you are strong in that skill and a way that you are weak. Then choose one goal for better communication.** To get them started, give an honest example of your own strengths, weaknesses, and goals.

Call for volunteers to share their goals. Do not pressure anyone. Encourage students: **During the rest of this session, look for actions and attitudes that will help you reach your goal.**

EXPLORING THE WORD

WORD PASSWORD

For each group of four, write these key words on individual cards: STUMBLE, PERFECT, BIT, RUDDER, TONGUE, SPARK, FIRE, EVIL, TAME, PRAISE, CURSE.

Divide into groups of four, seated so that two pairs face each other. Explain: **The one sitting across from you is your partner and the one next to you is your opponent. We will play a game of "Password" to search James 3:2-10. As you play, keep your Bibles open to James 3:2-10 to search for the passwords and clues that lead to them. The object of the game is to guess the words based on one-word clues your partner will give you. You'll take turns guessing and giving clues.**
1. The password giver shows one player from each team the word, and the first player gives his partner a one-word clue. If the partner guesses the word, the pair earns 10 points. If not, the second player gives his partner a clue and they earn 9 points for a correct answer. The point value goes down for each clue.
2. That round continues until someone guesses correctly or the point value is zero.
3. Another round starts with a new word. Alternate sides and alternate which pair gets to give the first clue.
4. All passwords are found in James 3:2-10. If a translation varies slightly but the player can show the word from his Bible, the guess will be counted correct.

OPTION: Instead of assigning password givers, let each team draw its own words and keep its own score.

When all teams have finished, point out: **You have focused on key words and now understand several truths from this passage.** Ask: **What truths do you notice about communication?** (Examples: Our TONGUES are hard to control; words can PRAISE or CURSE.)

Challenge your group: **Weigh every word before it leaves your mouth. Does it praise or curse? Be sure it praises!**

WHAT'S THE REASON?

Explain: **Many of the problems we have with our parents have nothing to do with their being our parents. Read James 4:1 and suggest some examples from everyday life.** After several responses, supplement with: **This verse explains that sometimes our own inner struggles cause problems with others. We want things that we don't have. Maybe we need the things or relationships we want, maybe we don't; but either way, they cause problems. You might be upset because you don't have a date, but you take it out on your parents. Your mom might be upset because a coworker got the promotion she wanted.**

Ask: **What other factors cause problems?** Encourage examples which have to do with being a teenager and those that don't.

Point out: **Sin itself is the cause of many of our problems. It's been said that if we all lived as God wanted us to live, we'd never have any problems. There's a lot of truth to that. James 4:7-8 encourages us to flee from the devil and draw near to God. As we understand God better and refuse to give in to the devil's schemes (such as "Go ahead and get even!" and "It doesn't matter how you treat them; they're your parents!"), our relationships with our parents tend to be smoother.**

Encourage your group: **Whenever you have a problem with your parents, look for the reason(s) and talk about it. Knowing the source of the problem helps you solve it.**

APPLYING THE TRUTH

IMAGINE GREAT COMMUNICATION

Direct youth: **Close your eyes and imagine the friend with whom you communicate most clearly. What makes this friend special? How do you know he or she understands you? Why do you feel free to share your thoughts and feelings with her or him?** Now distribute paper and direct students to write or draw the friends they imagined, making sure they use pictures, words, or symbols to depict the characteristics that make their friends good communicators.

Call for volunteers to hold up or read their images. Direct each to choose one characteristic from the picture and add it to a large COMMUNICATE acrostic which you have written on the chalkboard or poster board. Feel free to use each letter more than once if you have more than 11 students. This example has two for "U":

Care
Openness
Meaningful
co**M**mitment
Understanding, looks **U**nderneath the surface for the cause
Needs me and I need her
Interest
Concern
Agree on things at least some of the time
Takes time for me
fe**E**ls with me

If you have the student book, have each student choose one letter from "Spell Out Communication," explain the action/attitude that starts with that letter, and give an example of how to do it with his or her parents.

Challenge your teens to treat their parents with the actions and attitudes on the acrostic. Explain: **When you communicate well with your parents, they tend to communicate well with you.** But add: **In some situations, no matter how hard you try, parents don't respond. Reread James 4:1—the problem is likely something in their present or past that troubles them.** Assure your group that communication is a two-way street and that, though they are responsible *to* their parents, they are not responsible *for* their parents' behavior. They usually cannot change their parents.

A MATTER OF FRIENDSHIP

Ask: **Why do we tend to treat our friends better than our parents?** After several responses, highlight these ideas:
- You tend to show your worst (and best) side to people you live with the most. If you lived with your friends, you would tend to fight with them too.
- Because you feel at least some assurance that your parents will love you no matter how you treat them, you feel free to treat them however you want. You don't feel this safe with your friends—you know you must treat them well to keep them.
- It's hard to get along with people who have authority or power over you. You sometimes feel more like rebelling than working with them.

Challenge your group to treat their parents as they do their friends.

PRACTICE COMMUNICATION

Briefly review the discoveries made so far: **We need to practice a few of the principles we've learned. Let's review them:**
- **We've discovered four ways to communicate. What were they?** (Actions, attitudes, words, tone of voice.)

- **We've discovered some important things about our tongues. Who can name one?** (Examples: Hard to control; can bless or curse.)
- **We've learned to look for something behind every action. What was it?** (The reason.)
- **We've talked about characteristics of good communication. Who can name one?** Encourage several students to respond.
- **We've discovered one person we tend to communicate well with. When we treat our parents the way we treat this person, we'll tend to get along with them better. Who is this person?** (A friend.)

WORKOUT SHEET

Challenge your group to do some role-playing to apply what they've learned. Encourage them to act realistically.
1. Recruit two volunteers, one to play a parent and the other a teenager.
2. One volunteer draws from a bag containing the situation cards from Workout Sheet #4; the other draws from the reaction cards. If the "parent" draws the reaction card in this role play, have the "teenager" draw it in the next role play.
3. Together they try to deal with the situation and develop a positive reaction, using good communication *actions*, *attitudes*, *words*, and *tone of voice*.

Let the role plays continue for about 60 seconds (you may need to remind the players that their goal is to solve the problem, not make it worse) and then evaluate using such questions as:
- **How true to life was this role play?**
- **How might you improve any of the communication skills used?**
- **What did you learn about your parents by playing their role?**

Call on another pair to draw a situation and reaction. Repeat until five minutes before the end of the study. If you use up all the cards, just return them to the sack, shake, and repeat.

WHEN IT DOESN'T WORK

Ask: **What if you try all these communication actions and they don't work?** After several responses, supplement with these truths:
1. **Good communication never happens overnight. You will probably have to repeat the same actions over and over before seeing results. These results usually come gradually.**
2. **You can't change or be responsible for your parents' behavior. But your trying to communicate lovingly increases the chance that they'll try to communicate lovingly.**
3. **Don't use your parents' lack of response as an excuse for not trying, but don't feel guilty about it either.**

PRAYER FOR PEACE

Close by reading Romans 14:19 and by inviting your group to pray for Jesus' peace in their families.

TRADING GAME

Make one copy of this sheet for every group member. Cut the copies on the lines, creating cards to be traded.

ATTITUDES

TONE OF VOICE

ACTIONS

WORDS

ROLE PLAY CARDS

 Make one copy of this sheet and cut out the situation cards and reaction cards. Place the situation cards in one sack and the reaction cards in another. Direct volunteers to choose one of each and solve the situation in the light of that reaction. OPTION: Change reactions every 30 seconds.

SITUATION	SITUATION	REACTION	REACTION
Teenager wants to stay out 30 minutes past curfew.	Parent wants teenager to pick up his or her room.	Becomes angry.	Is in a bad mood because of something else.
Teenager wants to watch a movie that parent says teaches ungodly values.	Parent thinks teenager is playing his or her music too loud.	Is sick.	Says, "You don't understand!"
Teenager thinks parent points out too many dangers about parties.	Parent urges teenager to get along better with brother/sister.	Says, "You don't trust me!"	Accuses the other of a know-it-all attitude.
Teenager wants a piece of designer clothing that parent says is too expensive.	Parent prohibits a friendship with a person who uses drugs/alcohol.	Says, "You don't know what it's like!"	Says, "You don't realize what will happen if you do do that!"
Teenager wants larger weekly allowance.	Parent wants teenager to do homework before going out.	Doesn't want to compromise.	Says, "All you think about is money!"

PARENT PRESSURE

SOLVING CONFLICTS (Selected passages)

KEY CONCEPT

All teenagers have at least occasional conflicts with their parents, but most of these conflicts can be worked out.

MEETING THE NEED

This session will respond to the following student questions and comments:
- "Why can't my parents see things my way?"
- "My parents just don't see reality."
- "I'd rather live with my friends; they're easier to get along with!"

SESSION GOALS

You will help each group member
1. discover causes and solutions to family conflict,
2. examine conflicts in three Bible families,
3. speak about and practice conflict-solving skills.

SPECIAL PREPARATION

___ Bring extra Bibles, blank cards, pencils, chalk, large and small pieces of paper.
___ Bring a balloon for "Internal Pressures."
___ Bring the question can begun in session 1.
___ Write the Bible passages and post the questions for "Conflict Since the Beginning."
___ Encourage students to bring their Romans 14:19 cards from session 1.
___ Duplicate Workout Sheets #5 and #6 for each student. Cut apart an extra copy of #5.
___ Bring the student books if you have them.

BUILDING THE BODY

INTERNAL PRESSURES

Bring a large uninflated balloon. Invite group members to share conflicts they have with their families. (Examples: How late I can stay out; how much I'm responsible for at home; what I can watch on television.) Every time someone names a conflict, blow one breath into the balloon. Continue until the balloon bursts or students warn you that it will burst. Ask:

- **What happened (will happen) to this balloon when I keep blowing conflicts into it?** (It bursts; it is destroyed.)
- **What will happen to your family life if you continue to have conflicts that you never solve?** (Sample answers: Will grow apart; will burst apart; will be damaged.)

Emphasize: **Conflict between teenagers and parents is inevitable. But we don't have to let it destroy our relationships. Instead, let's learn to let out the pressure and solve the conflicts. That way we can continue to be close and keep from hurting each other. We can enjoy rather than destroy.**

CANNED QUESTIONS

Draw a few questions from the question can begun in session 1. Encourage the group to address them based on what you've studied so far. Supplement as needed. Consider researching any questions you haven't fully addressed. Encourage students to continue to add questions as they think of them.

LAUNCHING THE LESSON

I CAN MAKE A DIFFERENCE

Have your students write their names vertically on blank cards. Instruct them: **Next to each letter of your name, write a cause of conflict between you and your parent(s).** Supply the cards and pencils.

Example:
  D isappointment
  A ggravation
  N eed time alone

Compile the causes of conflict on the chalkboard or large paper. Point out: **Some of the causes stem from misunderstanding** (show an example from the list such as "My dad doesn't understand that I need my freedom"); **some stem from unmet needs** (example: "I have to make A's before my parents are satisfied"—unconditional love not met); **and some are sins** (examples: abuse, criticism). You may use the student book to clarify these categories. Agree that the categories are illustrative only and that many causes fit into more than one category.

Encourage your group: **By recognizing the causes of conflict as you have, you show tremendous insight and understanding. By using that same insight and understanding, you can be a part of the solution to conflicts between you and your parents.** Have them turn their cards over and write their names vertically again. This time they should write ways they can help solve conflicts. Example:

> **D** etermined to solve the problem
> **A** nger talked about
Recognize **N** eeds and meet them

Compile the suggestions for solving conflict as you compiled the causes. Point out: **You've suggested several ways to move from conflict causing to conflict solving. You've listed several actions which lead toward being honest about problems and working together to solve them. Professionals call these "conflict-resolution" skills. See how smart you are!**

Point out and repeat throughout the session: **It's crucial that you realize that you alone can't solve all the problems in your families. Solving conflicts takes two: you and your parents. You cannot control, nor should you feel responsible for, your parents' actions. But your actions will influence their actions at least a little, just as their actions influence you. In this session we'll concentrate on what you can change: your attitudes and actions; and we'll discover ways your attitudes and actions can help both you and your parents. Then we'll pray that God will work in your parents as He works in you.**

Review some of the last session's communication skills using the material in "Practice Communication" in session 2. Emphasize: **The closest families aren't those that have no conflict, but those that learn how to talk through conflicts and solve their problems.** Consider writing this on a poster or the chalkboard.

EXPLORING THE WORD

> ### CONFLICTS SINCE THE BEGINNING

Point out: **Conflicts have plagued families since the beginning of time. Even Adam and Eve blamed someone else when they ate the forbidden fruit. Let's discover some of the misconceptions, needs, and sins behind three Bible family conflicts.** Give each pair of students one of these Bible passages written on a slip of paper.
A. Genesis 4:2b-16
B. Genesis 37:2-8, 19-28
C. 1 Samuel 20:27-34 (for background read 15:26-28; 16:14, 21)

Post these four questions and guide students to search the passage for the answers.
1. What misconception(s) led to this conflict? What is the truth?
2. What unmet needs contributed to this conflict? How might the needs have been met?
3. What sins are behind the conflicts? How might they become aware of the sins and stop sinning?

4. When have you acted or been tempted to act like the characters in this passage (you can choose any character)? What were the results in your family? How might living by the truth help your situation go better than this one?

Encourage the group to share their findings. Sample answers (#4 will vary from student to student):

A. Genesis 4:2b-16.
1. Misconceptions: *Cain thought God wouldn't mind if he didn't bring his best.* The truth: *God does want our best.*
2. Unmet needs: *Cain's need for success was unmet because he brought an unacceptable offering.* Needs met: *Doing right brings acceptance (v. 6).*
3. Sins: *Jealousy toward Abel, which led to plotting against him, which led to murder, which led to lying, which led to trying to avoid God's question, which led to complaining against God.* Solution: *Cain could have talked about his anger with God (God invited him to do so) rather than let it lead to murder.*

B. Genesis 37:2-8; 19-28.
1. Misconceptions: *Joseph's dad thought it was all right to have a favorite.* The truth: *All children are equally important and parents should not play favorites.*
2. Unmet needs: *Joseph's brothers needed unconditional acceptance from their father.*
3. Sins: *Favoritism by the father; hate by the sons; murderous thoughts; selling into slavery; deceiving the father.* Solution: *Might have prevented the sins of hatred, murder, selling, and deceiving by talking to their dad about their needs and his favoritism; dad could realize his favoritism.*

C. 1 Samuel 20:27-34.
1. Misconceptions: *Jonathan thought his dad, Saul, didn't like his friend.* The truth: *Saul was jealous of David because Saul had given up the kingdom by deciding not to obey God.*
2. Unmet needs: *A good relationship between Saul and God; closeness and understanding between father and son; father's acceptance of son's friend.*
3. Sins: *Saul yelled at Jonathan (and insulted his mother) when it was really his own disobedience to God that had led to jealousy and anger.* Solution: *Saul could look at himself rather than blaming David and Jonathan; Saul could apologize to Jonathan; Saul could recall his disobedience, recognize his jealousy as wrong, confess, and ask God to help him do right.*

APPLYING THE TRUTH

PEACE AT HOME

Ask your students to pull out their cards (from session 1) on which they wrote Romans 14:19 and to repeat it together. Remind them that they made these cards two weeks ago. Some will have kept them in their billfolds and some will have posted them at home. Ask: **Who had opportunity to** practice this verse these past two weeks? What do the passages we have just studied suggest about creating peace at home?** Invite several to share. Add your own example from your family. Encourage your group to continue to look for opportunities to be peacemakers in their families.

WORKOUT SHEET

Shuffle the cards that you cut out of Workout Sheet #5. Explain: **I have in my hand several ways to solve conflicts. I'd like each of you to take one card and make a 60-second speech about that action or attitude. You might want to talk about why it helps solve conflict, when it's easy to do and when it's hard to do, or give an example of how to do it. You can say whatever you want to say about it. It's up to you! I'll take volunteers, but each of you will get to do one. Who would like to go first?** Affirm your students by smiling, nodding, and saying, "Good point!" Motivate reluctant speakers with such comments as: "It's only one minute," "I know you have good ideas," and "You can do it!" If you have more than 10 students, reshuffle the cards and use them again. Each speech can emphasize different points.

When all have spoken, review the points the students made. Give each group member a copy of Workout Sheet #5 as a reminder of skills they can use to solve conflicts with their parents.

WHAT'S THE NEED?

Explain: **Many sins in relationships occur because we decide to meet our needs the wrong way. For example, Cain needed to deal with his anger. But rather than talking about his anger and frustration, he took it out on Abel.**

If you have the student books, ask your students to find needs which tend to cause conflict if they are not met. Ask: **What other needs can you name? Can you give an example of a conflict each unmet need causes?** Jot these on the chalkboard as students name them.

If you do not have the student books, suggest or supplement with these samples: *When parents don't love unconditionally, they tend to demand that their teenagers act a certain way; when one doesn't respect the other's ideas, teens and parents tend to fight rather than understand; when kids aren't given some privacy, they often want to get out of the house; when parents don't have privacy, they might be grouchy; when teenagers don't get attention for positive behavior, they act out; when teens don't get admiration from parents, they might take drugs to get admiration from friends; when parents are disappointed about something that happened at work, they can be disagreeable at home.*

Ask: **What are some positive and destructive ways to meet each need?** Encourage several responses. (Example: Positive way to get respect is to ask for it and demonstrate that you're worthy of it; negative way is to demand your way or be a "man" in the worldly way, which includes drinking, rowdiness, sexual conquests, etc.)

PUTTING IT ALL TOGETHER

Hand out paper and pencils and have each student write a conflict he faces with one or both parents. (If they have trouble thinking of a conflict, suggest these idea-starters: My mom won't let me date; I want more attention than I get; I feel like my privacy is invaded; I think they tell the neighbors everything; their job/boat/car/ seems more important to them than I am.)

Collect and redistribute the papers with these instructions: **Write your understanding of the conflict by answering the first three questions we used during Bible study.**

WORKOUT SHEET

After a few minutes, pass out Workout Sheet #6 with these instructions: **Now follow the plan on this Workout Sheet to recommend a solution to the conflict.** Suggest that they also use some of the 10 skills they shared in their speeches.

Call on group members to read the conflicts, their understanding of them, and their recommendations. Encourage the rest of the group to contribute their ideas.

Encourage your students to take the Workout Sheet formula home and use it with their parents. The process is one that many seminar leaders use in teaching conflict solving. Stress: **This is a sample formula. Feel free to adapt it to what works best in your family.**

WORKING WITH GOD

Close with phrase prayers, coaching youth to: **Say one phrase at a time to God that tells a feeling, need, or praise about your relationship with your parents. Remember, only one phrase at a time: if you have more than one thing to say, wait until at least two others have prayed and then take another turn.** Silently count to 20 after the last one prays before closing the prayer. This gives reluctant members an opportunity to pray silently and maybe orally.

▶ CONFLICT-SOLVING SKILLS

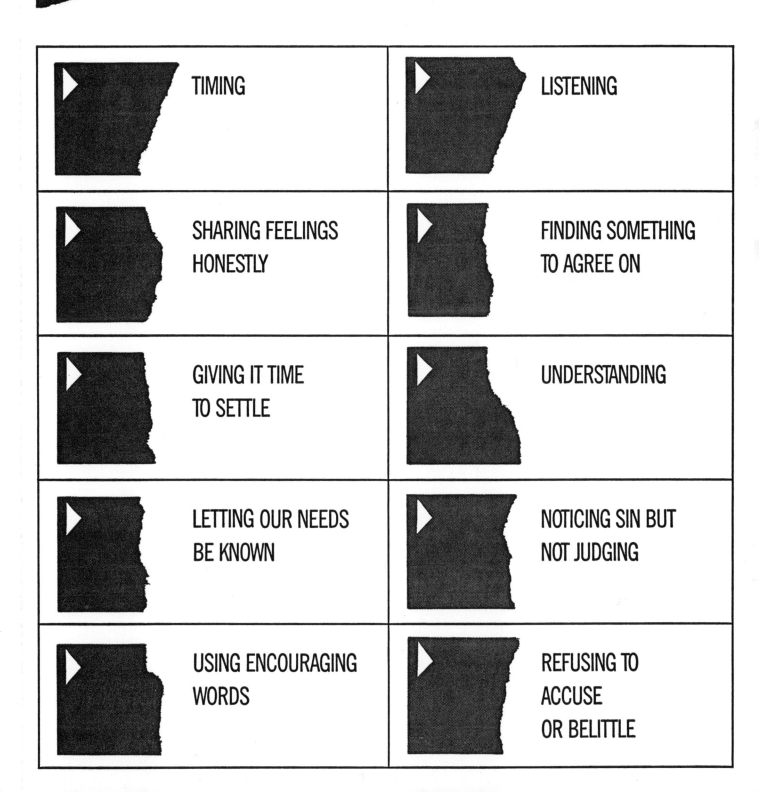

TIMING

LISTENING

SHARING FEELINGS
HONESTLY

FINDING SOMETHING
TO AGREE ON

GIVING IT TIME
TO SETTLE

UNDERSTANDING

LETTING OUR NEEDS
BE KNOWN

NOTICING SIN BUT
NOT JUDGING

USING ENCOURAGING
WORDS

REFUSING TO
ACCUSE
OR BELITTLE

Conflict-Solving Strategy

▶ For parents and teens to use together

1

DEFINE THE PROBLEM.

Example: *I* want to stay out later than you want me to stay out.

2

LIST SEVERAL SOLUTIONS (without evaluating).

Example: *Let* me stay out as late as I want to.
Let me stay out as late as my friends.
I'll come in whenever you say.
I'll live on my own so I can be my own boss.

3

EVALUATE THE SOLUTIONS.

Example: *The* second and third are the best possibilities.

4

CHOOSE A SOLUTION THAT PLEASES YOU BOTH.

Example: *We'll* get my friends' parents together and all agree on a curfew.

5

PUT THE SOLUTION INTO PRACTICE.

6

EVALUATE AFTER YOU'VE USED THE SOLUTION FOR AWHILE.

SESSION 4

BUILDING TRUST
(Ephesians 4:17-32)

Mutual trust builds closeness and prevents problems. Trust is both earned and given.

KEY CONCEPT

MEETING THE NEED

This session will respond to the following student questions and comments:
- "My parents don't trust me."
- "I don't trust my parents."
- "Why do I have to earn my parents' trust? Can't they just give it?"

SESSION GOALS

You will help each group member
1. share his or her experiences with and feelings about trust,
2. discover questions to ask about his or her actions,
3. select at least one action to increase trust in his or her home.

SPECIAL PREPARATION

___ Bring extra Bibles, pencils, 3" x 5" cards, markers, large and small pieces of paper, masking tape, and chalk.
___ Bring blindfolds for half the group for "Exercise in Trust."
___ Bring the question can and any answers you've researched.
___ Bring modeling clay for "The Shape of Trust."
___ Duplicate Workout Sheets #7 (one per person) and #8 (one per threesome).
___ Write the verses for "Question Your Trustworthiness."
___ Bring the student books if you have them.
___ Write out or duplicate assignments for "Youth/Parent Teamwork."

BUILDING THE BODY

EXERCISE IN TRUST

Set up an obstacle course in your meeting room and do not allow students to enter until half of them are blindfolded. Instruct each "seeing" student to select a blindfolded student and guide him or her through the obstacle course unharmed. If your group is uneven in number, participate yourself.

When the pairs reach the end of the obstacle course, instruct them to switch places: the seeing partners now become blindfolded and the blindfolded ones now see. The newly seeing students now guide their newly blindfolded partners back through the obstacle course.

Debrief the experience with such questions as:
- **How easy was it to trust your partner?**
- **Was it easier to trust before seeing the obstacle course or afterward?**
- **You who led and then were blindfolded, how did knowing what you knew affect how easy it was to trust your partner? Did your partner steer you away from any obstacles you had forgotten?**
- **Did anyone peek? Why?**
- **Did any guides let you bump an obstacle? How easy was it to trust after they let you bump?**
- **How does this exercise compare with your trusting your parents and your parents' trusting you?**

Supplement the comments with: **Sometimes we think we see well enough to guide ourselves, but we may be blinded in some way. Trusting our parents to guide us is seldom easy, even though they have had more experience.**

CANNED QUESTIONS

Draw a few questions from the question can begun in session 1. Encourage the group to address them based on what you've studied so far. Supplement as needed. Explain: **Though we could not discuss all questions as thoroughly as we would like, I hope we've helped answer your parent questions. Please feel free to come to me with any questions you'd like to talk about more completely.** If students come to you with questions you do not know how to answer, explain that you will get back to them after researching the answer. Then talk with your pastor or another person who can help you find the answer. You may even want to take the student with you to talk with your pastor or staff minister.

LAUNCHING THE LESSON

THE SHAPE OF TRUST

Give each student a piece of modeling clay. Instruct them: **Use your clay** to demonstrate trust. **Shape it into a symbol or image of trust. There are no right or wrong answers; your honest ideas are what count.** In response to "I don't know what to do!" just repeat the instructions and encourage with words like: "What shapes or images come to your mind when you think about trust? Shape the clay like those images."

Call for volunteers to show and explain their sculptures. Encourage them with comments like: **I like that shape—why did you choose it?** After each model say: **That really helps me understand trust better because. . . .** As you point out their insights, group members gain confidence in exploring God's truths.

NOTE: Leaders tend to skip a step like this one because it seems like play and takes up "too much time." But the insight young people share when they manipulate an object in their hands is amazing. They create their own object lessons. Don't hesitate to try it!

| **WORKOUT SHEET** |

Divide into groups of four. Give each student a copy of Workout Sheet #7 and a pencil, and say: **We've shaped our images of trust. Now let's share how we feel about it. Complete this sheet individually, circling the first answer that comes to your mind. Then each of you share your answer to number 1, each to number 2, and so on. After sharing each answer, tell why you chose it. Remember that there are no right or wrong answers. Your honest answer is the right one.** Circulate and encourage the groups to share honestly.

Explain: **Noticing our hopes and feelings about trust gives us a starting place for growth. Circle on your paper the area in which you most want to increase trust in your family. Then find actions during this session that will help you do that.** Have the students fold their Workout Sheets and put their names on the outside. Collect them, explaining that you will give them back unopened to use later in the session.

EXPLORING THE WORD

| *QUESTION YOUR TRUSTWORTHINESS* |

Ask: **Should trust be given or earned? Why?** When several students have responded explain: **Trust is both given and earned. We must show ourselves trustworthy to earn and maintain trust, but we must be given trust to have opportunity to show we can be trusted.**

Point out: **Just as with communication and conflict solving, trust is a two-way street: we can't make our parents trust us, nor can we insist that they act in ways that make it easy to trust them. But acting in trustworthy ways increases the chances that they will do both.** Pause to pray for both parents and the youth of your community, asking that trust might grow in each family.

Direct students to open their Bibles to Ephesians 4. Provide Bibles for those who did not bring theirs. Give these instructions: **Following the guidelines in Ephesians 4:17-32 insures that our actions will demonstrate trustworthiness. Draw a verse number from my envelope and write a question based on that verse—a question you could ask yourself to evaluate whether your action leads to trust. For example, after reading verse 17, I'd ask: "Does my action show futile (useless) thinking?"** Pass your envelope, which has these verse numbers inside (duplicated if you have more than 12 students): 18, 19, 22, 23, 24, 25, 26, 27, 29, 30, 31, 32.

Call out each verse in order, asking whoever has that verse to suggest a question based on it. Enlist one student to write the questions on the chalkboard or large paper. Point out: **Verses like 29, 31, and 32 suggest several questions. What other things could you ask?** Samples:

- v. 18—Where is my understanding darkened? Am I hardening my heart?
- v. 19—Where am I showing insensitivity? Am I indulging in something dangerous?
- v. 22—In what way might I be deceiving my parents or myself?
- v. 23—Does my attitude show my new life in Christ?
- v. 24—Does my action imitate God?
- v. 25—Am I telling the truth without twisting it?
- v. 26—Am I letting my anger lead to sin? What sin?
- v. 27—Where might I be giving the devil a foothold?
- v. 29—Are my words encouraging or destructive?
- v. 30—Does what I do or say make the Holy Spirit sad?
- v. 31—What evidence of bitterness or anger am I demonstrating?
- v. 32—How am I being kind and compassionate? Am I showing forgiveness?

Give each student a 3" x 5" card on which to write three questions to serve as checkpoints of personal trustworthiness. Suggest: **Think of an easy way to remember them, such as spelling a three-letter word.** Example:

Am I **T** elling the truth without twisting it?
    A re my words encouraging or destructive?
    D oes what I do make the Holy Spirit sad?

Ask a volunteer to read Ephesians 5:1. Ask: **Why is imitating God the essence of trustworthiness?** Summarize their comments and suggest: **Ask yourself: Would Jesus do this? If so, you can do it with a clear conscience, and you'll likely earn trust from your parents.**

WAYS TO GAIN TRUST

Call on a volunteer to read Ephesians 6:2. Ask: **What is the promise that comes to those who obey this verse?** (That it will go well with you and you will enjoy long life on the earth.) Ask: **What does it mean to honor?** Encourage as many synonyms as possible. (Examples: Esteem, admire, acknowledge, respect, accept, think highly of.)

Point out: **Honoring parents is the most powerful way to gain their trust. How can we do this? First let's name ways to lose trust.** Group students in threes to list 10 ways to lose their parents' trust. Provide paper and pencils. If you have the student books, suggest that they search chapter 4 for ideas.

As students report their ideas, compile them on a large list. (Examples: Lie; twist the truth; say, "It doesn't matter just this once"; sneak out; go where you've been told not to go; talk back.)

Compliment the students on their perception. Then instruct the same trios to list 10 ways to gain trust. Direct them to the student books for ideas.

Once again compile a large list. (Examples: Tell the truth; discuss your disagreement with your parents rather than disobeying; complete your chores during the time allotted; demonstrate your Christian beliefs in ways parents can see, like the way you treat siblings.)

Discuss the two lists with questions like:
- **Which is easier: to gain or lose your parents' trust?**
- **Why do we find it so tempting to disobey our parents?**
- **What can we do when we genuinely think our parents' instructions are wrong?**
- **How can we honor our parents when we disagree with them?**
- **What if our parents don't act in ways that deserve honor?**
- **How might honoring our parents help them become the parents God wants them to be?**

STUDENT BOOK OPTION

If you have the student book, direct your group to search "Trust Gets Complicated" for fears and unmet needs that contribute to lack of trust. Ask: **What other factors harm or help trust?** (Examples: Mood; what other teenagers in the community are doing; past behavior.)

Point out that trust is more complex than "I trust you" or "I don't trust you." Encourage youth: **Look beneath the surface to find out why your parents may be having trouble trusting you, or why you're having trouble trusting them.**

APPLYING THE TRUTH

WORKOUT SHEET

While students are still in groups of three, instruct them: **I want you to act as a "family" for the next several minutes. Designate one person as the father, one as the mother, and one as the teenager.** After a moment to decide, give each "family" a copy of Workout Sheet #8 and read through the instructions. Circulate to be certain that each situation has been chosen by at least one family group. If you have more than four groups, point out that two groups may have the same situation but will probably solve it differently. (OPTION: Let each family group write its own situation.)

After a few minutes, call for the family groups to act out their solutions. After each role play, encourage discussion with such questions as:
- **Parents, how did it feel to be in the parents' position?**
- **Teens, how did it feel to be in your position?**
- **What other suggestions would you offer for solving this dilemma?**

WHAT I'LL DO

Return Workout Sheets #7 to their owners. Direct your students: **Based on what we've studied in this session, write next to your circled area of growth one action and one attitude you can take to earn and keep your parents' trust. Then refold the papers and place them in your Bible, pocket, or purse.** Challenge them to increase trust in their homes by doing as they have written.

YOUTH/PARENT TEAMWORK

To review this unit, emphasize: **Everyone's family life has difficulties and problems. We've studied reasons these problems occur, ways to clarify communication, conflict-solving strategies, and actions that build trust. To summarize and help us remember what we've learned, choose one of these positions:**
● REFEREES: Write a manual for Christian family life. Include the name of the coach, rules for play, fouls and penalties, and exercises that strengthen playing ability.
● ADVERTISING CREW: Create a slogan and banner which shows why working toward happy family life is worth the effort.
● SPORTS REPORTERS: Write a newspaper story about a "Most Valuable Parent" (MVP). Tell why this parent is important to you and how he or she works with you to create a happy relationship.
● RADIO/TELEVISION COMMERCIAL: Using the tune of a popular television or radio commercial, write a commercial explaining actions and attitudes teenagers can take to create a happy family life.

After reading each assignment, allow each student to select one. Encourage them to keep the teams even. Display copies of the assignments, and supply paper and markers. (Team size should be three to five. If your group is small, offer only the assignments you most want to emphasize. If your group is large, duplicate teams.) Encourage teams to draw on information from this session and the prior three sessions in this unit.

Call for the teams to present their creations. Point out something positive about each. Consider duplicating or displaying their creations for your church. Explain: **Through this activity, you have pinpointed ways teenagers and parents can work toward God's ideal of family happiness.** Encourage them to live what they have discovered!

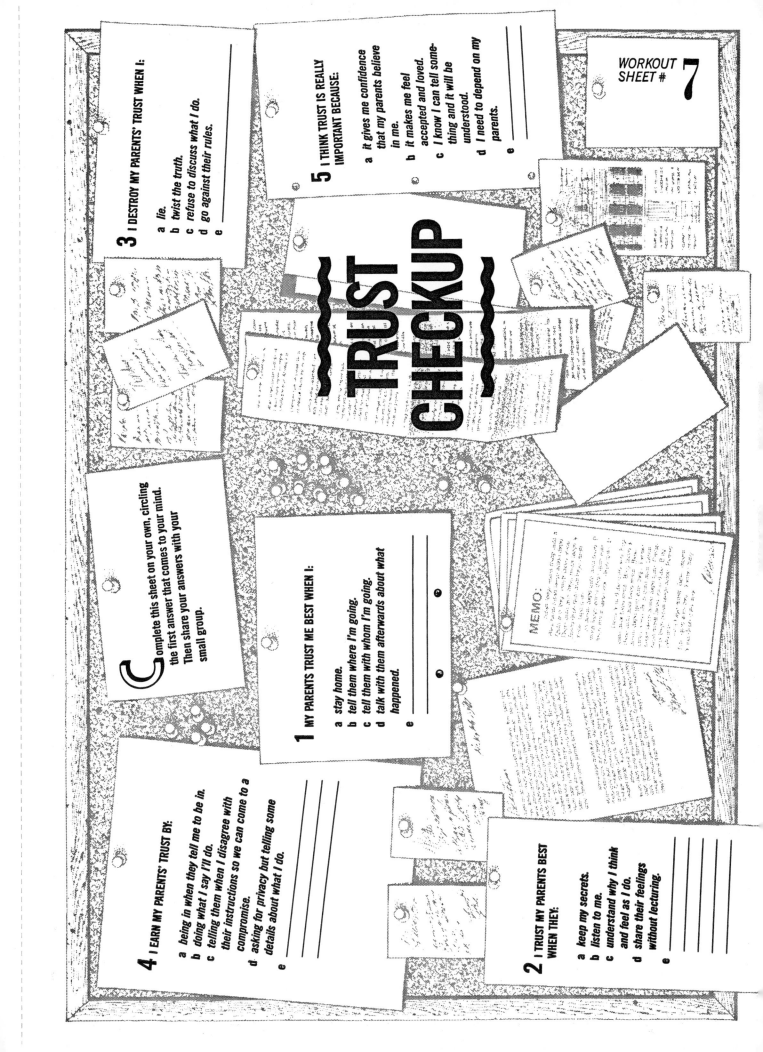

TRUST CHECKUP

Complete this sheet on your own, circling the first answer that comes to your mind. Then share your answers with your small group.

1 MY PARENTS TRUST ME BEST WHEN I:

a stay home.
b tell them where I'm going.
c tell them with whom I'm going.
d talk with them afterwards about what happened.
e _____

2 I TRUST MY PARENTS BEST WHEN THEY:

a keep my secrets.
b listen to me.
c understand why I think and feel as I do.
d share their feelings without lecturing.
e _____

3 I DESTROY MY PARENTS' TRUST WHEN I:

a lie.
b twist the truth.
c refuse to discuss what I do.
d go against their rules.
e _____

4 I EARN MY PARENTS' TRUST BY:

a being in when they tell me to be in.
b doing what I say I'll do.
c telling them when I disagree with their instructions so we can come to a compromise.
d asking for privacy but telling some details about what I do.
e _____

5 I THINK TRUST IS REALLY IMPORTANT BECAUSE:

a it gives me confidence that my parents believe in me.
b it makes me feel accepted and loved.
c I know I can tell something and it will be understood.
d I need to depend on my parents.
e _____

MEMO:

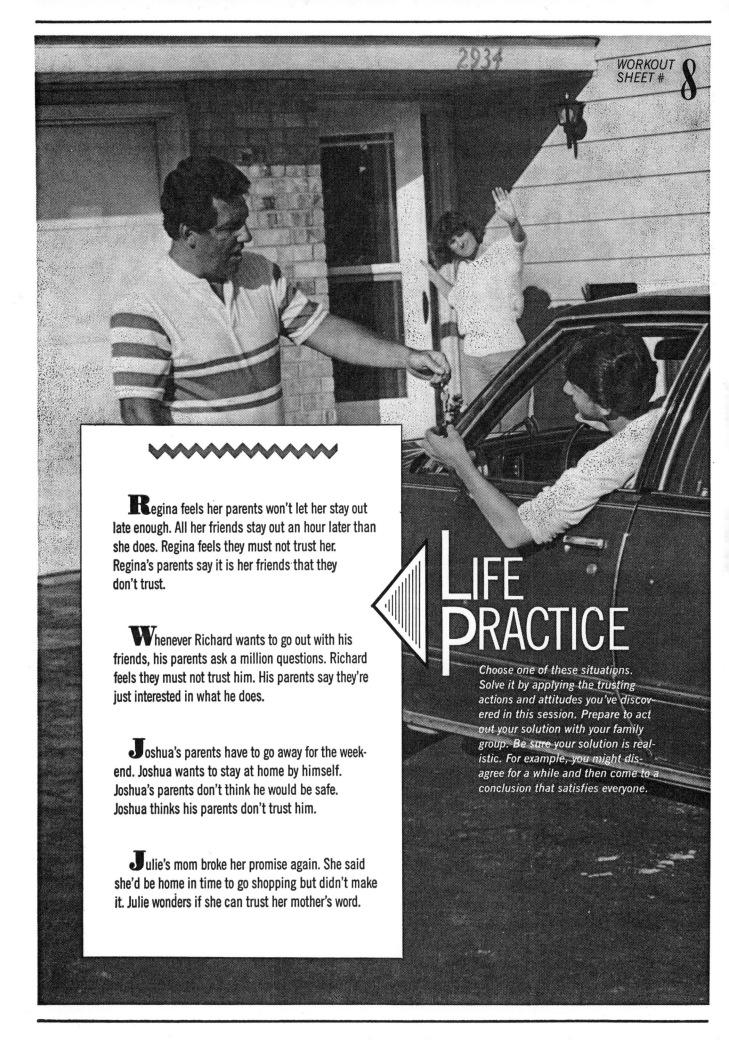

〰〰〰〰〰〰〰〰〰

Regina feels her parents won't let her stay out late enough. All her friends stay out an hour later than she does. Regina feels they must not trust her. Regina's parents say it is her friends that they don't trust.

Whenever Richard wants to go out with his friends, his parents ask a million questions. Richard feels they must not trust him. His parents say they're just interested in what he does.

Joshua's parents have to go away for the weekend. Joshua wants to stay at home by himself. Joshua's parents don't think he would be safe. Joshua thinks his parents don't trust him.

Julie's mom broke her promise again. She said she'd be home in time to go shopping but didn't make it. Julie wonders if she can trust her mother's word.

LIFE PRACTICE

Choose one of these situations. Solve it by applying the trusting actions and attitudes you've discovered in this session. Prepare to act out your solution with your family group. Be sure your solution is realistic. For example, you might disagree for a while and then come to a conclusion that satisfies everyone.

HOME IS WHERE THE HEAT IS

All young teens live in less-than-perfect families, but increasing numbers of teens experience the more obvious problems that result from divorce, death, blended families, and non-Christian parents. Though their pain may be no worse than the pain youth from "intact" families experience, these young teens *feel* that their families are less holy, less normal, less acceptable. As a result, *they* feel less holy, less normal, and less acceptable. They tend to let these feelings draw them away from God and the church, rather than toward the very ones who can comfort and heal them.

This unit addresses issues raised by divorce, single-parent homes, blended families, and families with at least one non-Christian. Not all your students will be in all these situations, but all will know someone who is. Motivate your group to create a loving atmosphere where these sensitive issues can be discussed openly and with the guidance of the Holy Spirit.

Remember, several of the sessions suggest more activities than you may have time to do. This allows you to choose what works best for your group. If one teaching approach does not appeal to you or meet your students' needs (and you know them best), you will still have enough material to fill your session. Even though you may not use all the material, prepare for all or most of it in case you have extra time.

SESSION 5

DEALING WITH DIVORCE (Matthew 19:3-9; John 4:4-30)

KEY CONCEPT

The church can be a source of healing and wholeness for the pain that divorce causes parents, their teenagers, and their friends.

MEETING THE NEED

This session will respond to the following student questions and comments:
- "Because my parents are divorced, people in church don't like me."
- "I wish I had a normal family."
- "My friend's parents are getting a divorce. What can I do?"

SESSION GOALS

You will help each group member
1. accept that divorce does not decrease one's worth in God's eyes,
2. aim toward God's ideal of lifelong marriage,
3. support those experiencing family pain.

SPECIAL PREPARATION

____ Bring extra Bibles, pencils, markers, large and small pieces of paper, masking tape, and chalk.
____ Duplicate Workout Sheets #9 and #10. Cut apart Workout Sheet #9 to make a deck for each group member.
____ Prepare and display the "Jeopardy" game for "Exploring the Word."
____ Bring the student books if you have them.
____ Write out the instructions for "Guide to Healing Family Pain."
____ Review minilecture so you can present it naturally.

BUILDING THE BODY

HELP FOR THE WOUNDED

As students enter, direct them to stations equipped for four people. At each station post these instructions: **Pretend one person in your group has a broken limb (leg or arm). Bandage that person and then prepare to act out ways you would help that person while the injury heals.** Provide large paper, tape, and markers at each station.

After several minutes, call for each group to dramatize ways they would help their injured friend. List the helping actions on the chalkboard or large paper as groups act them out. Encourage the audience to clap loudly for the group with the most helping actions.

Discuss the experience with such questions as:
- **Why does the friend need help?** (The limb won't do its usual tasks.)
- **Why are friends important at a time like this?** (Can help the injured person keep on living happily; can include them when they might get left behind.)
- **How is this experience like helping friends cope with divorce?** (Friends need us; we can help them get through a painful time.)

Emphasize: **Divorce injures the emotions just as fractures injure the bones. The healing is easier with friends who care. Divorce is never good, but when it happens we can be instruments of God's love.**

LOOKING FOR THE GOOD

Have each member, starting with you, share one good thing about his or her family. No one may repeat what another has said. After going around the circle, explain: **We all have problems in our families, whether our parents are divorced or not, whether our problems are obvious or invisible. But we all also have good in our families. Focusing on the good can give us strength to handle the bad.**

LAUNCHING THE LESSON

WORKOUT SHEET

Give each student a deck of sins created by cutting apart a copy of Workout Sheet #9. Direct them: **Stack these sins in order of severity. Separate from the deck any actions that are not sins at all.**

Call for several volunteers to attach their cards in order to a bulletin board or wall. Ask: **Why are there so many different possibilities? Which list is right?** (No one ordering will be more correct than another.) **What actions did you discard from your stacks? Why? How can you tell whether something is a sin?** (Example: Hurts us or someone else; God forbids it.)

Explain: **Sin causes pain for self, for others, for God; God forbids sin because He wants our happiness, not because He wants us to feel bad. God does not reject us when we sin.** Ask: **Now, would you change the way you have ordered your stack or add any other cards to it?**

Briefly explain: **All these actions are sins. Divorce is certainly a sin, but it is no worse than other sins that people commit. Because the consequences of divorce are obvious and far-reaching, we sometimes set it up as one of the "big" sins and use it as a test of faith or friendship.**

Emphasize: **People rank sins. God doesn't. Like God, we can accept the sinner without accepting the sin. The church can be the place where divorced families find the love, encouragement, and support they need to get through the trauma and pain of divorce. The church can help them move toward family happiness.**

EXPLORING THE WORD

BIBLE JEOPARDY

To study the two Bible passages, play a variation of the game "Jeopardy." Prepare the game before the class by writing the following answers on individual 8-½" x 11" pieces of paper. Write the Bible reference and sample question on the back of each answer. Display the answers in three rows, in order of point value, with the category taped above each row. Cover each answer with a second piece of paper that has its point value written on it. You may want to enlist a student to help you prepare the game. (If you cannot post the answers give them orally.)

Category: QUESTIONS

Points	Answer	Sample Question
10	The question Jesus asked the woman at the well.	What is "Will you give me a drink?" (John 4:7)
20	The first question the Samaritan woman asked Jesus.	What is "How can You ask me for a drink?" (John 4:9)
30	The question the Samaritan woman asked the townspeople.	What is "Could this be the Christ?" (John 4:29)
40	The question the Pharisees asked to test Jesus.	What is "Is it lawful for a man to divorce his wife for any and every reason?" (Matthew 19:3)
50	The question the Pharisees asked about the Old Testament	What is "Why then did Moses command that a man give his wife a certificate of divorce?" (Matthew 19:7)

Category: WORDS OF JESUS

Points	Answer	Sample Question
10	The way Jesus sent the Pharisees to the Bible for answers.	What is "Haven't you read . .?" (Matthew 19:4)
20	The way Jesus told the Samaritan woman that He is the Messiah.	What is "I who speak to you am He"? (John 4:26)
30	What Jesus said about His water.	What is "Whoever drinks the water I give him will never thirst"? (John 4:14)
40	How Jesus told the Samaritan woman He knew about her divorces.	What is "The fact is, you have had five husbands"? (John 4:18)
50	What Jesus said about marriage.	What is "What God has joined together, let man not separate"? (Matthew 19:6)

Category: BIG WORDS

Points	Answer	Sample Question
10	The people Jews won't associate with.	Who are Samaritans? (John 4:9)
20	Religious leaders.	Who are Pharisees? (Matthew 19:3)
30	The Creator's goal for marriage.	What is "one flesh"? (Matthew 19:5)
40	The reason for divorce.	What is marital unfaithfulness? (Matthew 19:9)
50	The one who will explain everything to the Samaritan woman.	Who is the Messiah (Christ)? (John 4:25)

Explain: **On the wall are three categories with five answers in each category. This is a game of Bible Jeopardy based on Matthew 19:3-9 and John 4:4-30. As we play, you'll learn about the passages because you have to read them to play. Keep your Bibles open to Matthew 19:3-9 and John 4:4-30. These are the rules:**
- **The person with the birthday nearest to today will choose the first category and point value.**
- **I will remove the point card to reveal the answer. The first person to stand asks a question which matches the answer and tells the verse where she got the answer.**
- **If that person is correct, she keeps the point card. If not, the next person standing gets a chance to try.**
- **The correct questioner chooses the next category and point value.**

- **All answers come directly from Scripture. You must show in your Bible where you found the question.**
- **If there is more than one correct question, _____ will be the judge who decides whether a question matches an answer.**

Play until all questions are correctly given. The person with the most points wins. Note that all who played won Bible knowledge.

Ask: **How would you summarize these two passages in one sentence?** (Example: Jesus wants lifelong marriage but loves us even when we don't achieve it.) Encourage several students to respond and then review these truths:
- Jesus taught that lifelong marriage is what God wants.
- Building a lifelong marriage definitely brings the greatest happiness to both parents and their children.
- When a couple fails to achieve lifelong marriage, God still loves them.
- Jesus showed His love for the woman who had been divorced five times.

APPLYING THE TRUTH

| *WORKOUT SHEET* |

Ask: **If lifelong marriage makes both people and God happy, why does divorce occur?** After students have shared several ideas, distribute Workout Sheet #10 and read through the instructions.

After a few minutes, ask volunteers to make 30-second speeches about the reasons they chose. Encourage all to try, and always give lavish praise afterward, even if only a bit was said. If two choose the same reason, suggest that each talk about a different aspect of that reason.

Explain: **Knowing the causes of divorce is the first step to preventing it in your own marriage. You cannot change your parents' marriage, but you can change your own.** Ask: **How can we work toward lifelong marriage?** As the group brainstorms, list their ideas on the chalkboard or large paper. Highlight ideas from the list. Add comments like:
- **Marriage is work, and the best marriages aren't those without problems, but those in which there is commitment.**
- **Marriage is not like in the fairy tales. "Happily ever after" isn't automatic.**
- **You can practice for marriage by talking out problems with friends and by learning to get along with all sorts of people in all sorts of situations.**
- **Choosing dates who share your values minimizes conflict and increases the chance of compatibility.** Ask: **What are some ways you should definitely be alike?** (Examples: Both Christians; similar church background; respect for each other; lifestyle goals.)

| *FROM TEEN TO TEEN* |

Read this letter from a teenager to encourage your students to work toward happy marriages:

I've seen what happens when my parents don't work through their problems. Before we marry, I want my fiancée and me to make a commitment to try to resolve any problems, instead of quitting and giving up. I realize marriage is not all fun and games, and if I marry someone who knows that, maybe we can learn to live with each other. We'll listen to each other rather than accuse.

I've already been praying that God would guide me to the one He wants me to marry and that I'll abide by God's decision. I don't think my parents started that way. I know that even Christians get divorces, so I'm working toward permanence.

Although I don't like to think about it, if my wife decides to divorce me, I know I'll have God on my side, and as He says, His grace is all we need.

STUDENT BOOK OPTION

Enlist two volunteers to read the letters in chapter 5. As the letters are read, direct the rest of the group to underline feelings they experienced when their parents divorced, or think they might feel if their parents would divorce.

Ask: **What needs do the teenagers in these letters have?** (Examples: Expressions of love from both parents; acceptance by church; friends who will listen and care.)

Which of these needs might you meet, and how? (Examples: Understanding—by listening; friendship—by telling her I'm glad she's my friend and by spending time with her.)

How can we uphold God's goal for lifelong marriage and still accept divorced people? (Examples: Jesus accepted divorced persons, so we're following His example; do it just as we accept other sinners without accepting their sin; learn how to create lifelong marriage for the future.)

GUIDE TO HEALING FAMILY PAIN

Point out: **None of us can make it through family problems alone. If your parents are divorced, talk about it with an adult or same-age friend that you feel comfortable with. And whether or not your parents are divorced, you can be the friend a "divorced" teenager needs.** Guide trios of youth to design a "Guide to Helping Friends with Family Pain." Provide paper and pencils. Write on the board these suggested categories:
1. What to do
2. What not to do
3. Words and actions that help and heal

After trios have worked on their lists for a while, explain: **I'd like to share some information that might give you more ideas for your guide. As I talk, take notes on your guide (do's, don'ts, and words or actions).**

MINILECTURE

Present the following information:

● Kids in divorced or blended families agree that what helps them most are friends they can talk to. So the most important thing to do is listen. Questions you might ask to encourage your friend to talk are: *How have you been feeling about your parent's divorce? What do you think will happen next?* Assure your friend that you are there to listen whenever he or she needs you.

● Everyone who goes through divorce experiences grief, and expressing grief is necessary for adjusting to the divorce. The grief process is predictable, and understanding it can help you get through it yourself or help a friend through it.
1. The first stage is denial: The person can't believe the divorce has actually happened. During this stage, listen and agree that it's hard to believe. Don't be harsh about forcing your friend to face the facts. She's not ready yet.
2. Second comes deep emotion: Some express it through crying, others through anger at their parents or at God, others through feelings of depression and hopelessness. You can stand by your friend by being there, by accepting emotion, by crying with him, by sending cards that say "I care," by not insisting that he snap out of it.
3. Finally—and it may take up to a year or more—your friend accepts the divorce. He or she will never like the divorce, but will feel ready to move on. Again, listen, be there, go places together, and assure your friend that whenever feelings about the divorce come, you're there to listen.

Instruct the teams to complete their guides and to read portions to the group.

NOTE: This "Guide to Helping Friends with Family Pain" will be the first of a four-chapter "guidebook" called "Guide to Healing Family Pain." In each session of this unit, the students will add a chapter to the guidebook. Feel free to create four separate guides or to combine them into one four-chapter guide. Consider duplicating a version combining the whole group's work to distribute to the church or to a sister church youth group.

PRAYER

Close by praying a prayer like: **God, please give us the courage, skill, and motivation to work toward Your goal of lifelong marriage. And give us also the grace to forgive ourselves and others when we or they fall short of that goal. Thank You that Your love meets all our needs.**

D **Getting Drunk** D

M **Murder** M

L **Lying** L

V **Vandalism** V

C **Criticism** C

D **Divorce** D

S **Stealing** S

C **Cussing** C

R **Revenge** R

G **Gossip** G

A **Adultery** A

M **Making fun of People** M

STACK-
~ING
◇ THE
DECK

CUT

these cards apart and stack them in order from the least sin to the greatest. Remove from the stack any actions which are not sins.

Why Does *DIVORCE* Occur?

If divorce causes so much pain, why do people do it? Just as in physical death, marriages die for many reasons. Select the reason you think is most often true or write another reason that you think is important. Then doodle, draw, or write why you think that is the main reason for divorce. Feel free to jot ideas under the others after you've worked on your main choice.

Divorces occur because people don't understand that all marriages have problems. They split rather than solving their problems.

Divorces occur because people don't know that love is something you create, not something that just happens.

Divorces occur because television, music, and other media present it as an easy solution to marriage problems.

Divorces occur because no one supports the family anymore.

Divorces occur because jobs or other commitments receive more attention than the marriage. Then the marriage relationship grows weak and dies.

Divorces occur because one or both stop trying.

Divorces occur because _____

SESSION 6

ONE PARENT AT MY HOUSE (Selected passages)

KEY CONCEPT

Single-parent homes provide extra challenges for all family members.

MEETING THE NEED

This session will respond to the following student comments:
- "I miss my other parent so much."
- "I wish I had a normal family."
- "I feel guilty because I have both parents."

SESSION GOALS

You will help each group member
1. identify problems unique to single-parent homes,
2. pinpoint strengths that can help in handling the extra challenges of a single-parent home,
3. identify actions that help create family happiness.

SPECIAL PREPARATION

____ Bring extra Bibles, pencils, markers, masking tape, and chalk.
____ Duplicate Workout Sheets #11 and #12.
____ Bring paper for "Collecting the Problems" and "We're All Part of the Family."
____ Bring the student books if you have them.

BUILDING THE BODY

COMPLETE THE CHALLENGES

For each team, prepare an envelope containing several challenges that can best be accomplished by two people. Examples: Carry one of your teammates across the room by forming a two-person armchair; move a large table from one side of the room to the other; hold a 60-second conversation about the pleasures and difficulties of getting along with parents; write a list of 10 benefits of living in a family.

Divide the group into teams of about 5. Give each team an envelope and instruct them: **Race to complete all the challenges in your envelope before the other team(s) finish(es). Half the challenges may be done with two people, but the other half must be completed by only one person.**

Discuss the experience with these questions: **Why was it easier to complete the challenges with two people?** (Shared the load, etc.) **Could the jobs be done by one person?** (Yes; for example, could carry the teammate on back instead of in two-person chair.) **How are one-parent households like completing the challenge with one person instead of two people?** (Examples: Can still do the job but it's harder; one parent must think through things independently rather than discuss them.)

Explain: **Through death, divorce, or never having been married, single-parent families are created. They're no less valuable than two-parent families, but they create extra challenges. Working together, kids and their single parents can meet the challenges and create family happiness.**

WHAT I LIKE ABOUT MY PARENTS

Encourage every member of the group to say one thing he likes about one of his parents. No one may repeat exactly what another has said. After going around the circle, explain: **All of us have frustrations with our parents, whether there are one or two parents in our homes. Focusing on what we like about our parents can encourage us to work with them to create family happiness.**

LAUNCHING THE LESSON

WORKOUT SHEET

Break into groups of four. Give each student a copy of Workout Sheet #11. Direct them: **Circle or draw the symbol that best describes your relationship with one of your parents. Then when I call time, take turns**

showing your group the symbol you chose, and why.

After the groups have shared, ask sensitively, **Who of you have only one parent living at your house? How were your problems similar to or different from those with two parents living at their house?** Encourage all to participate in this last question. Summarize, using student's own points and statements like: **Having one parent doesn't make much difference in some types of problems. For example, almost every teenager has some trouble communicating with his or her parents. Having one parent presents some unique problems, such as your parent's loneliness. Having two parents also presents unique problems, such as your parents' struggling to agree on how to run the home. As we talk about homes with one parent, let's remember that all homes have problems. Let's encourage each other to face whatever challenges our homes present.**

STUDENT BOOK OPTION

If you have the student books, direct students: **In chapter 6, circle the greatest frustration you face as a member of a single-parent home, or that you think you would face if one of your parents died or moved away.**

Guide members to share their choices with their groups. Then instruct them: **Now for each frustration, name a way a two-parent family might experience a similar frustration. For example, children of two-parent families might spend a lot of time alone if both parents worked long hours.**

Point out: **Noticing that our feelings are similar can help us be sensitive to each other and to learn how to help each other create family happiness.**

COLLECTING THE PROBLEMS

Give each student two pieces of paper and a pencil. Instruct them: **Write on each piece of paper a problem you have with one parent, whether both live in your home or not. We'll use these anonymously at the end of the session. Include as much detail as you want to include.** Collect the problems and save them for use during "A Story About Making Your Family Happy."

EXPLORING THE WORD

WORKOUT SHEET

Point out: **Homes with one parent can be happy or sad depending on how the family members handle the extra challenges. Workout Sheet**

#12 lists several situations that Ishmael and his single mother, Hagar, faced. Complete section A of the sheet by reading Genesis 16:1-15 and 21:9-21 and filling in the verses that tell about each experience.

Review the answers (1 = 16:5-6; 2 = 16:7-12; 3 = 21:9-14; 4 = 21:15-16; 5 = 21:17-19; 6 = 21:20).

Then explain: **Ishmael's single-parent situation was an extreme example. Hagar bore a child for Sarai, a type of surrogate-mother situation that created more problems than it solved. But God took care of Hagar and her son Ishmael. Many of our single parents were not always single. Some of them became single because of death or divorce. But no matter how our families were created, truths from Ishmael's life can encourage us.** To find out how these truths can encourage, instruct students to complete section B of the workout sheet by matching Ishmael's situations with the situations that affect them.

Read the statements from the bottom of Workout Sheet #12 and encourage students to call out the situations/verses that match (correct order: 1, 5, 3, 2, 4, 6). Emphasize that God will meet our needs no matter what happens in our families.

WE'RE ALL PART OF THE FAMILY

Call on a volunteer to read Ephesians 3:14-21 as all students follow in their own Bibles. Ask: **Where is the word "family"?** (Verse 15.) Explain: **All Christians belong to a forever family, the family of Jesus Christ. Because we belong to this family, Jesus will take care of us in all circumstances. As I read this passage again and again, doodle to illustrate the truths you hear.** Hand out paper, and read the passage about three times. Call on volunteers to show and explain their doodles.

Highlight the students' ideas and supplement with such comments as:
● Verse 16 explains that Jesus will give us power.
● Verse 17 explains that we have roots in love.
● Verse 18 says that we have the power to understand.
● Verse 19 says that Jesus' love fills us completely.
● Verse 20 reminds us that Jesus enables us to do even more than we imagine.
● Verse 21 explains that all the good that happens to us in our families can bring glory to God.

Ask: **According to these verses, how does Jesus help us face our family situations?** (Examples: Power; family feeling; understanding of parent's feelings; understanding why we feel the way we do.)

Ask: **Who would like to share how Jesus has helped you deal with a family predicament?** Encourage but do not force group members to share.

Explain: **Becoming part of Jesus' family begins when you become a Christian. I encourage you who have not yet become Christians to** do so. **Simply tell Jesus you accept His love and want Him to guide your life. Please talk with me or another Christian adult you trust about your decision. We want to encourage you and share your joy as a new believer. I'll be here after class if you'd like to talk today.** Be sure to remain a few minutes and be accessible when class concludes.

APPLYING THE TRUTH

> ## *A STORY ABOUT MAKING YOUR FAMILY HAPPY*

Summarize: **Of course we all want families with two parents who love each other and who love us. But because of death, divorce, and past problems, that is not always possible. These disappointing events hurt, but they don't have to destroy our family happiness forever. No matter what has happened to your family in the past, you can work toward the joy that comes when all family members work together to meet each other's needs in the name of Jesus Christ.**

Let's imagine what this would be like by passing a story. We'll tell a group story about a family with one parent. Each of you will add a sentence to the story when your turn comes. From time to time, I'll add the problems that you wrote at the start of this session (during "Collecting the Problems"), **and you'll continue the story with ways our imaginary family solves them.**

Encourage students to be realistic with the story. Let the family act and react like a real family would. Students might even include a bad solution followed by a positive one, and should feel free to add other problems when their turn in the story comes. Explain that you will go around the circle several times (or until you feel the story is complete). Pause for questions and then start the story: **"Once upon a time there was a family with one parent. . . ."**

(A sample of how the story might go in the first several additions: "This family had two sons, a daughter and a father. . . . The mother had been killed in a car accident one year before. . . . The dad missed the mom so much that he refused to talk about her. . . . This created tension because the children wanted to talk about her to ease their own grief . . . so the children talked to each other. . . . The oldest son had to take care of the two younger ones after school. . . . He wished he could join a sports team like his friends. . . . He talked to his dad about this. . . . His dad shouted that he had to work every day, so why wasn't the son willing to help? . . . Later they talked some more and the dad finally agreed that he could join one sport a year if he would take care of the younger ones during the other seasons. . . .")

Keep in your hand the problems from "Collecting the Problems" and introduce them from time to time, being careful not to reveal the writers.

After several rounds, point out the group's good work and encourage them by saying: **Notice the many ways you have suggested for coping with problems with one parent!** Quickly jot them on the chalkboard as you and students recall them. Instruct them: **Take a moment to jot a few of** these down for use in your own home.

Comment further: **Happy endings are not limited to stories. We can help make our families happy whether we have one or both parents in our homes. How might we do this?** (Examples: Consider the other's needs; listen; understand; realize that parents aren't perfect and have needs similar to ours; find adult support outside home if you need it.)

Ask: **How can you work as teenagers to avoid being single parents?** (Examples: Pray that I'll listen to God's guidance in my dating and will recognize His choices for me; avoid teen pregnancy so I won't create a single-parent home myself; learn to solve problems rather than depend on divorce as an option.)

Emphasize: **No matter how hard you work to prevent it, you might end up as the head of a single-parent household. Many single-parent families are created when a spouse dies or when one parent is away on military service. How can we prepare for this?** (Examples: Know that our security is in God; do many of the loving actions we've already recommended for our current single-parent homes; trust God for the future; develop good friendships in church so we won't feel lonely.)

Say positively: **I encourage you to recognize your present family problems as challenges rather than reasons to be depressed. Approach your challenges head on, asking for God's wisdom and understanding as you work on them. There are no instant solutions, but your efforts can contribute to the likelihood of a solution rather than the certainty of failure.**

GUIDE TO HEALING FAMILY PAIN

Choose one of these options to form a second chapter to the "Guide to Healing Family Pain" begun last session:
1. Include the list of suggestions that came out of "A Story about Making Your Family Happy."
2. Tape-record "A Story about Making Your Family Happy" and enlist a student or your church secretary to transcribe it.
3. Write sample solutions for the dilemmas in "Practice Makes Perfect" in the student book.

MORE THAN WE COULD ASK FOR

Call on a volunteer to reread Ephesians 3:14-21 as a closing prayer.

PICTURE YOUR FAMILY

After circling the item in each group that best describes your relationship with your parent, share your answers with your group. Each of you tell your answer to number 1, then each to number 2, and so on.

1 Circle the symbol that illustrates something good about your relationship with your parent:

2 Circle the object that most closely illustrates your family communication:

3 Circle the mathematical sign that illustrates your closeness with your parent:

+   =   -   ✕   ÷

4 Draw a picture of your biggest problem with your parent:

5 Draw a picture of a solution that has helped that problem in the past:

GOD WILL TAKE CARE OF ME

God cares about your family. Genesis 16:1–15 and 21:9–21 tell about God's care for one single mother and her son.

Write in the verses that tell about each experience Ishmael and his mother faced.

_____ 1 Sarai became jealous and was so cruel to Ishmael's mother that Hagar ran away.

_____ 2 God heard Hagar's cry of distress, and sent His angel to explain that He would take care of them.

_____ 3 Teenage Ishmael and his mother were sent away by Sarah and Abraham.

_____ 4 Hagar feared that Ishmael would die of dehydration.

_____ 5 God provided water and promised to stay with Ishmael as he grew.

_____ 6 Ishmael grew to be a skillful hunter.

Now match Ishmael's situation to each of these statements that might affect your life.
Fill in the blanks with the numbers from the sentences above.

_____ Sometimes I feel like running away.

_____ God will meet all my needs and will help me grow up happy.

_____ Sometimes I or my parent get rejected.

_____ God knows my sadness and will take care of me.

_____ I have fears about my future.

_____ I can grow to be skillful in my job and in my future family.

HOME IS WHERE THE HEAT IS

TWO FAMILIES INTO ONE (Selected Bible promises)

KEY CONCEPT

Blended families present unique challenges in addition to the problems any family faces.

MEETING THE NEED

This session will respond to the following student questions and comments:
- "Why do I have to put up with her? She's not my *real* sister!"
- "Why couldn't my dad just have stayed single?"
- "Why is life harder since my parents remarried?"

SESSION GOALS

You will help each group member
1. imagine (or chronicle) life in a blended family,
2. apply Bible promises to family problems,
3. write a "Blended Family Survival Guide."

SPECIAL PREPARATION

____ Bring extra Bibles, pencils, paper, markers, masking tape, and chalk.
____ Choose and prepare relays.
____ Write and display the "Meeting the Need" statements.
____ Bring large paper or obtain chalkboard and chalk.
____ Duplicate Workout Sheets #13 and #14. Cut apart a copy of #13 for every ten students.
____ Bring the student books if you have them.
____ Braid three short strands of yarn for each student. Tie the ends.

BUILDING THE BODY

MEETING THE NEED-PART 1

Before class, write the three "Meeting the Need" statements ("Why do I have to put up with her? She's not my *real* sister!" "Why couldn't my dad just have stayed single?" "Why is life harder since my parents remarried?") on three sheets of paper and hang them from the ceiling. Give each student a piece of paper and marker as he or she enters. Instruct them: **Write a question you have asked about your blended family or would ask if you lived in a blended family. Then hang it from the ceiling with this masking tape** (or string).

A GAME PLAN

Play several relays that require cooperation from all team members. Examples: Carry each team member across the room in a chair; get each team member over a large obstacle; gather signatures from entire team; run three-legged (or four or more) races by lining up teens and tying their touching legs together.

Discuss the experience with these questions: **How important was working together? Who took charge? What difficulties did you have cooperating? How did you work out your difficulties? How is this experience like living in a blended family?** (Examples: Family must cooperate to complete everyday tasks; working together enables everyone to win; sometimes it's hard to work with other people.)

MEETING THE NEED-PART 2

Challenge the students: **Choose a question hanging from the ceiling and answer it. You don't have to answer it completely, just offer a suggestion. These are big questions!** Encourage discussion of the questions, but, if students start "chasing rabbits," gently close the discussion by pointing out that you'll cover the questions in more detail during the rest of the session.

Explain: **All of us are touched by blended families. Either we or someone close to us belongs to one. As we work together, we can help each other find answers to our questions and solutions to our problems.**

LAUNCHING THE LESSON

PASS THE STORY

Arrange the chairs in one large circle. Continue the "pass the story" format which closed last week's session, except let group members add the problems spontaneously. Give these instructions: **What's it like to live in a blended family, a family in which the children are related only by their parents' marriage? Imagine you live in a family like this or think about your own blended family experience. Together we'll tell a story about a family we create. We'll include the family's problems and pleasures. I'll start the story and you continue it, one sentence per person. We'll go around the circle several times.** Begin with this sentence: **"Once upon a time there were two single parents with children. They fell in love and married. . . ."**

Encourage students to suggest problems, solutions their imaginary family finds, and pleasures they have. If you have the student book, point out the sample problems under "Let Your Problems Become Challenges."

After several minutes, summarize the story elements with: **Life in a blended family is like an adventure: there are positives like [something a student said] and negatives like [something a student said], frustrations like [something a student said] and successes like [something a student said]. Let's discuss these and more in this session.**

A ROUND OF PROBLEMS

Give these instructions: **Let's go around the circle one more time; say your name and a family difficulty that starts with the letter or sound your name starts with. I'll write them on the chalkboard** (or large paper) **as you state them.** If a student struggles for more than 10 seconds suggest these options: A: anger; B: boring family activities; C: communication; D: dealing out responsibilities fairly; E: everyone wants attention; F: Fs on report cards; G: girls get privileges; H: half sisters are favored by stepparent; I: it's too crowded; J: jealousy; K: kids lots younger than I; L: laws set by new parent; M: move to new house; N: new school because of move; O: often have to care for younger siblings; P: parents seem more concerned with each other than with me; Q: quality time is hard to get; R: responsibilities I don't want; S: spontaneity is not as easy; T: time with my parent is less than it used to be; U: understanding someone new is hard; V: very hard to accept new family; W: wish my dad were still alive; X: extra grandparents; Y: yearn for____; Z: zzzzzz—not enough sleep.

Referring to the list on the board, ask: **Which of these are unique to blended families?** Circle those. **Which are similar to those that would happen in any family?** Star those.

Point out: **Blended families present unique challenges, and we'll address some of these in this session. We'll refer back to this list.** Leave the list displayed throughout the session.

EXPLORING THE WORD

WORKOUT SHEET

Write on the chalkboard these five Bible references: Lamentations 3:22-23; 2 Corinthians 4:8-9; Philippians 4:19; 2 Corinthians 1:3-4; Proverbs 3:13-14.

Duplicate a copy of Workout Sheet #13 for every 10 students and cut it apart. (Note the correct matches before you cut them.) Give each student one card.

Say: **On the chalkboard I have written the references to five Bible promises that can help us with blended family needs. You have in your hand half of one of those promises. When I say "GO," find the person who has the other half of your Bible promise. Write the Bible reference on your card using the list on the chalkboard. Then sit down with your partner and jot down one or more ways that promise can help with one of the circled problems on the board.** (Problems are from "A Round of Problems.")

Call for each pair to read their suggestions. Congratulate them on their good work.

Sample answers:
- Lamentations 3:22-23 reminds me that God will find me new friends in my new school. Because His compassions are new every morning, I know each school day will go well.
- Second Corinthians 4:8-9 lets me know that no matter how frustrated or confused communication gets at home, I won't be destroyed. I'll make it with Jesus' help.
- Philippians 4:19 lets me know that even though I miss my dad who died, God will give me people who will meet the needs he used to meet.
- Second Corinthians 1:3-4 helps me realize that because Jesus has understood me when I'm upset, I can understand my new family members.
- Proverbs 3:13-14 reminds me that God will give me the wisdom to say things so my parents will understand why I want quality time with them.

MEMORIZE FOR LIFE

Encourage the group to memorize the five promises on Workout Sheet #13 by singing them to a familiar tune. Instruct each pair: **Most of us can repeat commercial jingles without effort simply because they have been set to music. Let's memorize our Bible promises the same way. I'd like each pair of you to suggest a tune to which we can sing the Bible promises you matched. The tune can be a commercial, a currently popular song, or a hymn.**

After a minute or two, call for pairs to tell their suggested tune. Then say with encouragement and enthusiasm: **We'll now sing the verses to these tunes for our first memory practice!** Sing each verse as a group. Have fun! Challenge students to select one verse they will memorize this week.

WORKOUT SHEET

Enlist a volunteer to read Ecclesiastes 4:9-12. Display a length of yarn and challenge two students to pull it until it breaks. Then call on a volunteer to braid three lengths of yarn together and challenge the same two students to break it. Ask: **How much harder was it to break the three-stranded cord?**

Point out: **Families can provide these togetherness benefits when they work together. Blended families sometimes have to work harder to braid together, but their closeness can be just as binding and powerful. Let's write letters to God talking with Him about our families, whether blended or not. Using this Workout Sheet form, write what your family is now and a bit of what you'd like them to be.** Give each student a copy of Workout Sheet #14 and a pencil.

Call for volunteers to read their letters. Explain that writing a letter to God is a way of praying. Compliment students' genuine communication with God.

APPLYING THE TRUTH

GUIDE TO HEALING
FAMILY PAIN

Direct trios of students to create a third chapter to the "Guide to Healing Family Pain" called "Blended Family Survival Guide." Say: **Create a "Blended Family Survival Guide" dealing with issues like:**

FEELINGS OF COMPETITION	**LIVING IN TWO PLACES**
DISCIPLINE	**MOVING**
CHURCH REACTIONS	**CHANGING ROLES**

Suggest that groups fold their papers in half lengthwise and then in thirds the other direction to form six boxes to write advice about the six categories. If you have the student book, encourage students to search chapter 7 for ideas. After a few minutes, call for groups to read and explain their Blended Family Survival Guides.

STUDENT BOOK OPTION

If you have the student book, guide students to write letters of advice to the two teenagers in the first paragraph: one to the teen talking and one to the visiting stepsister. Suggest using truths learned during this session. Provide paper and pencils.

TWO ARE BETTER
THAN ONE

Call on a volunteer to reread Ecclesiastes 4:9-12. Give each student a piece of tri-braided yarn as a reminder of the truths in this verse.

UMAN MATCH CARDS

OUT these cards apart and give one to each student. (If you have more than 10 students, duplicate matches; if you have fewer than 10, choose your favorites or play more than once.) Instruct each to find the person with the other half of the Bible promise. (Currently correct matches of Lamentations 3:22–23; 2 Corinthians 4:8–9; Philippians 4:19; 2 Corinthians 1:3–4; Proverbs 3:13–14.)

Because of the Lord's great love we are not consumed . . .

. . . **f**or His compassions never fail. They are new every morning; great is Your faithfulness.

We are hard pressed on every side . . .
perplexed . . .
persecuted . . .
struck down . . .

. . . **b**ut not crushed;
. . . but not in despair;
. . . but not abandoned;
. . . but not destroyed.

And my God will . . .

. . . **m**eet all your needs according to His glorious riches in Christ Jesus.

Praise be to the God and Father of our Lord Jesus Christ, the Father of compassion and the God of all comfort, who comforts us in all our troubles . . .

. . . **S**o that we can comfort those in any trouble with the comfort we ourselves have received from God.

Blessed is the man who finds wisdom, the man who gains understanding . . .

. . . **f**or she is more profitable than silver and yields better returns than gold.

Dear God,

Two are better than one in my family because . . .

My family helps me up when I . . .

_____ threatens to overpower me
but my family helps me defend myself by . . .

My family is like a cord of three strands because . . .

Something else I'd like to tell you about my family is . . .

Sincerely,

"Two are better than one, because they have a good return for their work: If one falls
down, his friend can help him up . . . . Though one may be overpowered, two can defend
themselves. A cord of three strands is not quickly broken."
Ecclesiastes 4:9–12 (NIV)

SESSION 8

I'M THE ONLY BELIEVER (2 Timothy 1:1-14)

KEY CONCEPT

Extra encouragement and understanding from friends at church can help Christian teens in non-Christian homes feel less alone.

MEETING THE NEED

This session will respond to the following student comments:
- "I'm the only Christian in my family."
- "My brother says I'll outgrow this silly Christianity."
- "I feel weird at church because they always talk about families and my family doesn't come."

SESSION GOALS

You will help each group member
1. tell about times he has felt alone in his family,
2. identify actions that encourage deeper faith rather than frustration,
3. embrace the importance of seeking a Christian marriage partner.

SPECIAL PREPARATION

_____ Bring extra Bibles, a chalkboard or large paper, pencils, writing paper, and chalk or markers.
_____ Bring 40 balloons for "Find Support for Your Building"
_____ Duplicate Workout Sheets #15 and #16.
_____ Bring the student books if you have them.

BUILDING THE BODY

MIRROR IMAGE

Instruct students to line up according to hair color, from blondest to darkest. Fold the line at the halfway point so each teenager now faces another teen. Direct them: **Imagine you are mirror images of each other. The line I point to will move its hands, and the opposite line will move its hands exactly as the partner does.** Point to one line and then the other so each has an opportunity to both lead and follow.

Discuss the experience with such questions as: **How easy was it to move exactly as your partner did? What difference did the speed of movement make? How is this exercise like obeying Jesus?** (Examples: We watch and imitate His actions; even when we want to, we might have trouble obeying; it's fun to obey Jesus.)

Explain: **Being the only believer can make you feel like you can't follow movements in your family. You may feel lonely or different. Jesus understands these feelings. He is always here to help you recognize the source of your frustrations, to be your guide, and to show you what to do in even the most difficult circumstances.**

FIND SUPPORT FOR YOUR BUILDING

Divide the group into two teams and the room into two halves. Mark the dividing line with masking tape and check that both sides have approximately the same equipment (such items as chairs and hymnbooks to support tower). Give each team 20 balloons. Challenge them: **Your goal is to inflate your balloons and build a tower taller than the other team's. You can use anything on your side of the room to support your tower (including your own bodies) but the base and all layers of the tower must be of balloons. Notice that the room has been divided in half with this piece of masking tape. You are not to cross this line for any reason.** Encourage teams as they work, and promote enjoyable teamwork.

Congratulate the team with the tallest tower. Ask: **What did you use to keep your tower from tumbling or blowing over?** (Examples: Hymnbooks; people; chairs; wall.) **What forces threatened your tower?** (Examples: Gravity; shape of balloons resists stacking; other team blowing tower over; breeze in room.) **How is building this tower like being the only Christian in your family?** (Examples: No one to help you hold up your tower of Christian faith; parents might intentionally or unintentionally knock down your growth in Christ; need Christian friends to help you build your faith.)

Summarize the experience using students' own points and ideas like these: **The Christian life is like building a tower. Each experience can help us grow closer to what Christ wants us to be. Sometimes we feel like the forces against our growth are greater than the forces for our** growth, especially when the people we live with every day don't believe in Jesus. But we can always find support and protection against opposing forces. We find this in our church, our Sunday School, from Christian friends. And just maybe, as we build our Christian lives, our other family members will join us in beginning and building a life with Jesus Christ.

LAUNCHING THE LESSON

ONLY BUT NOT ALONE

Point out: **Kids who are the only Christians in their homes are extra special! They've had the courage to take a stand for Jesus even though someone close to them might not understand. We'd like to applaud those of you who have done that! Who has at least one non-Christian parent or sibling in your home?** Pause while students raise their hands. **We're proud of you, and though you know it already, we want to emphasize that Jesus will never let you down. You've made the right choice by choosing to follow Him.** Encourage thunderous applause!

Now we want to express pride in the rest of you: *anyone* **who becomes a Christian has made a great stand. And all of us need each other's support as we learn to live as Christians in our homes. Let's commit to encourage and understand each other, whether our parents are Christians or not.**

We want you who have not yet become Christians to join our family. With Jesus you always have a place to belong. Talk with me or someone else in this group about how to join Jesus' forever family. Be certain to linger after class.

Have the group stand and hold hands or, if they are comfortable, put their arms around each other. Pray something like this: **Jesus, we thank You that as Christians we have a place to belong. We thank You that we belong in this youth group and that we can encourage and support each other. Guide each of us to show our care for the others.**

OTHER REASONS FOR LONELINESS

Explain: **Being the only Christian in your family is just one reason you may feel alone in your home. We'll focus on this situation, but for a moment let's examine other circumstances that might make you or a friend feel very alone in a family. What are some of these?** Write ideas on the chalkboard. If the group has not already stated them, add these causes for loneliness: frequent family fights, emotional abuse, physical abuse, both parents work or are gone frequently, incest, alcoholism, excess parental demands, stormy communication.

Direct students to choose one of these situations and tell why they would make someone feel lonely, by spelling out that word. Provide paper and pencils. For example, "fights" could be spelled:

When my parents **F**ight
        I feel that I somehow must be at fault
   I **G**et embarrassed and am afraid to
      Have friends over because if my parents fight then,
      They (my friends) might like me less.

Explain: **There are solutions to all these problems. Jesus provides them. Be certain to tell an adult you trust about family problems that make you feel afraid or alone. You never have to suffer by yourself. Jesus will always be there for you, and loving church friends can help or point you to someone who can.** Assure your group that all families have problems and, because of Jesus and the church, no one has to hurt alone. Read Hebrews 4:15-16.

EXPLORING THE WORD

YOUR SPIRITUAL HERITAGE

Point out: **Every Christian heard about Jesus from someone else. Who told you about Jesus?** Direct youth to close their eyes and think about the person or persons who told them about Jesus. Allow 60 seconds of silence with eyes closed, then encourage a number of students to share briefly. Help them share details with questions like: **What did the person say or do that first interested you in Jesus? What doubts did you have at first? What words or actions did the person do to encourage you to accept Jesus?** Point out: **These people are part of your spiritual heritage, your roots: they are the ones who led you to Christ, who encouraged you in your faith, and may still serve as models for Christian growth. In many ways they are your spiritual parents. Some of you learned about Jesus from the parents who live in your home; many of you did not. But we all have spiritual roots, a heritage we can be proud of.**

To lead naturally into the Bible study say: **Paul, whom the Holy Spirit used to write much of the New Testament, encouraged a young believer named Timothy to look to his spiritual roots. According to 2 Timothy 1:5, who were these two people?** (His grandmother Lois and his mother Eunice.) Point out: **As far as we know, Timothy's dad was not a Christian; nor were Paul's parents Christians. Paul's parents were devout Jews and Timothy's dad was a Greek. Paul encouraged Timothy in his faith and Timothy grew to be a great Christian leader.**

WORKOUT SHEET

Give each student a copy of Workout Sheet #15, a pencil, and these instructions: **This crossword puzzle will guide us to discover some ways to grow our Christian faith. The puzzle is based on 2 Timothy**

1:1-14, part of a letter of encouragement from Paul to Timothy. The letter was written near the end of Paul's life, while he was in prison for teaching about Jesus. You may work on the puzzle with a partner. Circulate and encourage students as they work.

To review the answers, instruct students: **Circle the statement that suggests an action you could take to encourage another believer. For example, I would circle 4 down: "Like his forefathers, Paul served God with a clear *conscience."* I chose it because when I serve God, that encourages others to serve Him too.** Pause while students circle. Then explain: **We'll check the answers to the problem by letting you read your statement filled in with the correct answer.** Call for each to read his or her circled statement, telling why he or she chose it. Check off answers as they are read. Call for volunteers to fill in any answers not chosen. (ACROSS: 3. grace mercy peace; 7. Jesus; 9. Timothy; 10. son; 11. believed; 12. sincere; 14. Lois; 15. life. DOWN: 1. flame; 2. prayer; 4. conscience; 5. Paul; 6. ashamed; 8. Holy Spirit; 13. Eunice.)

APPLYING THE TRUTH

GUIDE TO HEALING FAMILY PAIN

If you have the student book, direct your students to search chapter 8 for ideas for a "Growing as a Believer in Your Home" guide. Write the following topics (and portions of the student chapter that apply) on the board to get them started:
- Ways to show your family that Jesus makes a difference in your life. ("A Fine Art" in the student book.)
- Needs or misunderstandings that might keep a parent from accepting Jesus. ("What's Behind the Resistance?" in the student book.)
- Where/how to find support from other Christians. ("When They Don't Believe" in the student book.) You might want to list names and phone numbers or at least blanks for each person to write his own list.
- Why it is important to pray for and search for a Christian mate. ("When They Don't Believe" in the student book.)

If you do not have the student book, brainstorm ideas and encourage students to arrange them in the guide.

Notice that "Growing as a Believer in Your Home" is the last section of a four-part guidebook called "Guide to Healing Family Pain." Each session of this unit has added a chapter. Consider duplicating a version combining the group's work to distribute to the church or to another youth group.

WORKOUT SHEET

Emphasize: **God doesn't have any grandkids. Each of us decides for himself whether or not to become a Christian:**
- **Some who become Christians have Christian parents. It definitely helps to have their support.**

- **Some who have Christian parents never become Christians.**
- **And some who do not have Christian parents become Christians.**

To emphasize the family-in-Christ-relationship, read the litany on Workout Sheet #16. Ask those born between January and June to read the boldface lines, and those between July and December to read the light copy.

Encourage the group to add to the litany by expressing other feelings about faith and parents, and responding to the feelings expressed.

ADVICE TO MYSELF

Point out: **We've studied divorce, single-parent families, blended families, and now being the only believer at home. We can't change the choices our parents made, but we can determine our own future choices. How can we prevent or at least lessen the likelihood of our own divorce or unhappy marriage?**

Supplement student ideas with these:
- Because only God knows the future, ask for His guidance both in your life and in the life of the one He wants you to marry. Pray that He'll equip both of you for the challenges ahead.
- Become happy in Jesus. The strongest families are created by those who don't need more money, more friends, more anything to be happy.
- Choose carefully the people you date and run around with.
- Realize that marriage is work. It's hard to learn to live with someone, so decide to learn how to care, to talk, to create happiness for each other.
- Know that the grass is not greener on the other side. Remembering another relationship may make you wish you'd married that person, but recognize that you'd have just as many problems with him or her.
- Practice problem-solving: Talk out problems with your friends. Make sure you can solve problems with anyone you date seriously.
- Ask a trusted adult to tell you what she sees in your relationship. She'll notice things (both good and bad) that you might not see.
- Find couples with strong marriages who will encourage you in your early marriage years. Turn to these people for advice.
- Know that no matter what comes—death of your spouse, debilitating disease, tragedy—God will take care of you.

After students have shared several ideas instruct them: **Write yourself an advice letter detailing actions you will take to reach your goals for lifelong marriage. I'll mail these letters back to you in a month. When you finish, seal your letter in this envelope and address it to yourself.** Collect the letters and mark your calendar to mail them.

Say: **We can turn around the trend. One by one we can make it more popular to stay married than to divorce, more common to live together happily than to frustrate each other, more acceptable to obey God than to ignore Him. Let's do it!**

GOD ONLY KNOWS

Pause to pray a prayer of affirmation and request for guidance for present and future families.

Roots Crossword

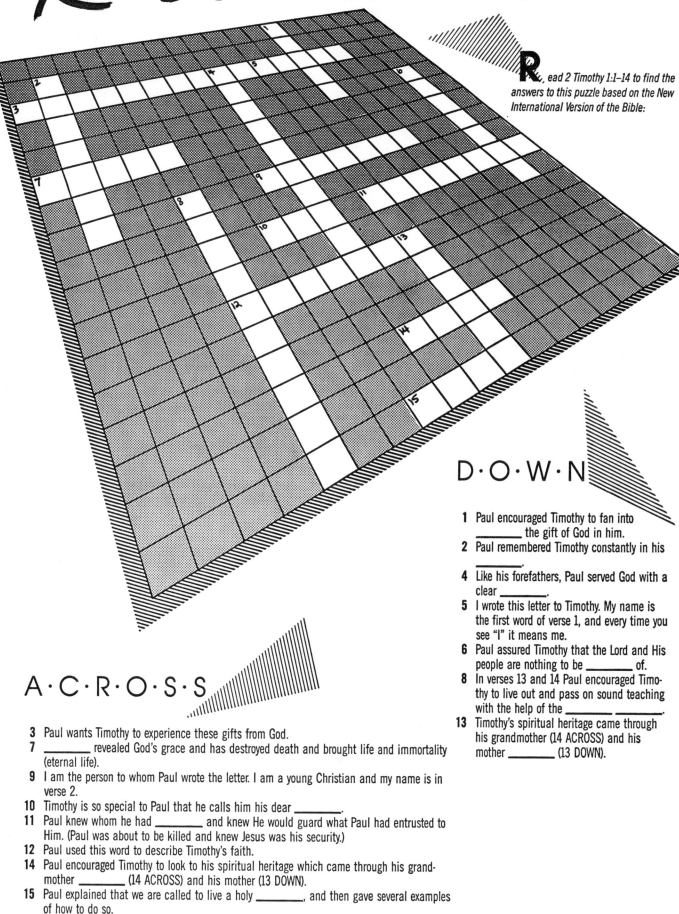

Read 2 Timothy 1:1–14 to find the answers to this puzzle based on the New International Version of the Bible:

D·O·W·N

1 Paul encouraged Timothy to fan into _____ the gift of God in him.
2 Paul remembered Timothy constantly in his _____.
4 Like his forefathers, Paul served God with a clear _____.
5 I wrote this letter to Timothy. My name is the first word of verse 1, and every time you see "I" it means me.
6 Paul assured Timothy that the Lord and His people are nothing to be _____ of.
8 In verses 13 and 14 Paul encouraged Timothy to live out and pass on sound teaching with the help of the _____ _____.
13 Timothy's spiritual heritage came through his grandmother (14 ACROSS) and his mother _____ (13 DOWN).

A·C·R·O·S·S

3 Paul wants Timothy to experience these gifts from God.
7 _____ revealed God's grace and has destroyed death and brought life and immortality (eternal life).
9 I am the person to whom Paul wrote the letter. I am a young Christian and my name is in verse 2.
10 Timothy is so special to Paul that he calls him his dear _____.
11 Paul knew whom he had _____ and knew He would guard what Paul had entrusted to Him. (Paul was about to be killed and knew Jesus was his security.)
12 Paul used this word to describe Timothy's faith.
14 Paul encouraged Timothy to look to his spiritual heritage which came through his grandmother _____ (14 ACROSS) and his mother (13 DOWN).
15 Paul explained that we are called to live a holy _____, and then gave several examples of how to do so.

WE'RE A FAMILY!

God, sometimes it gets lonely at the house I live in.

We're glad You're always there.

My parents don't always understand me.

We're glad You do.

I try to explain my love for You, but it doesn't always get through.

We're glad we don't have to explain our faith to You.

They tell me my beliefs are childish, that I'll outgrow them.

We know that Christianity is the only adult way to handle problems.

I wish there were other people who understood.

We do—we're your church, your youth group, your Christian friends.

I'm glad for people who understand.

Yes, we're a family—the family of Christ.

And maybe one day my family will believe too.

That's what we're all working toward.

In the meantime I'm glad for friends like you.

And we're glad for friends like you.

FAVORITISM, FIGHTS, AND RIGHTS

When two or more people live in the same household, conflict at some level is practically guaranteed. Each person will disagree with the other at least occasionally; one will irritate the other with pesky habits; one will want to talk while the other wants quiet; one will act unfairly toward the other, consciously or unconsciously. These minor irritants can become major problems if families do not develop ways to address them. The closest families learn to let the frustrations become catalysts for greater understanding and persistent loving. Because steady loving often seems like swimming against the tide, this unit attempts to strengthen young teens' family relationship muscles.

In too many families, teens may be the only ones working toward closeness. We need to admit this, not as an excuse for giving up, but to keep young people from taking on guilt that does not belong to them. Free your students to realize that, though it hurts, they alone cannot create family closeness. But they can continue to try, to create closeness in other relationships, and to work toward their own future family happiness. Pray together that all members of your students' families will commit themselves to happy family living.

PART THREE

FAVORITISM, FIGHTS, AND RIGHTS

SESSION 9

IT'S NOT FAIR!
(Philippians 2:1-11)

Christ-like humility brings more happiness than keeping score.

KEY CONCEPT

MEETING THE NEED

This session will respond to the following student comments:
- "My sister gets more privileges than I had at her age!"
- "Just because I'm younger, my mom treats me like a baby."
- "I have to mow the lawn while my dad watches the football game!"

SESSION GOALS

You will help each group member
1. illustrate unfair situations,
2. examine Jesus' attitude about His rights,
3. discuss feelings about humility and how to express it at home.

SPECIAL PREPARATION

____ Bring extra Bibles, markers, masking tape, pencils, paper.
____ Bring candy or pennies for the "Treasure Trade."
____ Plan games for "Keeping Score" if you choose that option.
____ Bring a huge piece of paper (rolled newsprint or several paper sacks taped together) for the "Unfairness Mural."
____ Duplicate, cut apart, and shuffle a copy of Workout Sheets #17 and #18 for each pair of students.
____ Bring the student books if you have them.
____ Obtain "Philippians Canticle" if you choose to use it.
____ Write the signs for "Agree/Disagree."
____ Write the marking directions for "Journal My Part."

BUILDING THE BODY

TREASURE TRADE

Give all group members the same five treasures. These can be candy, pennies, or another item of your choice. Challenge the group: **Your goal is to give your treasures away. You may give only one penny at a time to a person, and when a treasure is offered you must accept it.**

After about three minutes call time. Discuss the experience with questions like: **Did any of you succeed in giving away all your treasures? How did you do this? Did anyone hide or not socialize? What made it easy or hard to give away your treasures? To receive them? Why did the treasures seem to multiply?**

Point out: **Giving away treasures is like looking out for each other's interests. If we constantly look for ways to make the others in our family happy, there will be so much contentment, we won't be able to hold it all!** Agree that: **Of course no family does this all the time, but it's certainly worth striving for!**

KEEPING SCORE

Briefly play board games or indoor competitive games and keep score on a simple tournament chart.

After the games are over ask: **How did it feel to be on the loser's line(s)?** (Examples: Bad; embarrassing; wanted to go home.) **How did it feel to be on the winner's line(s)?** (Examples: Great; proud; wanted everyone to see my name.) Point out: **Keeping score helps only half of us feel good. Even the ones who win might feel bad because they feel sorry for the losers, or because their pride gets the best of them.**

Ask: **What would happen if we had a game where everyone could win?** (Some may say they would rather have a winner and that it would be dull without winners; others will say everyone winning would be great.) **How about in families?** (Some will say they'd rather win at all cost, or it's impossible for everyone to win; others will say it would be great.)

After several comments, supplement with: **Keeping score in families usually frustrates us more than it comforts us. When we worry about winning, we ignore the feelings of those we care about. Working together to solve family disagreements can help everyone win.**

LAUNCHING THE LESSON

UNFAIRNESS MURAL

Display paper the length of your room and instruct students to find a spot and draw an unfair situation that occurs in their homes or the home of someone they know. Stick figures are fine. Provide markers or crayons and encourage everyone to draw at the same time. Suggest the student comments listed under "Meeting the Need" at the beginning of this session as samples for those who may have trouble thinking of a situation.

When most people appear to be finished, call for volunteers to tell about their situations. Encourage empathy and understanding. Discuss the drawings with such questions as:
● Why is it hard to be fair in families?
● How does your age affect how your parents treat you?
● How do siblings affect the privileges and responsibilities you receive?
● Why does unfairness bother us so much?

Leave the mural on the floor and tell students: **When you hear an action or attitude that would solve one of these situations, write it around the picture. Keep a marker or crayon with you to add ideas as you hear them throughout the session.**

STUDENT BOOK OPTION

Ask two volunteers to read dramatically the dialogue between Marie and Edwin. After their dramatization ask: **When have you felt like Marie? Like Edwin? What might Edwin have said to help Marie rather than frustrate her? What options do you think Marie has?**

Emphasize: **You're not alone if you sometimes feel jealous or angry with others in your family. But these feelings quickly become sins if we don't deal with them. The Christians at Philippi must have had similar feelings, because Paul gave them advice for dealing with person-to-person struggles. He advised them to focus on Jesus and His purposes: like-mindedness, love, and oneness.**

EXPLORING THE WORD

WORKOUT SHEET

Direct students to choose a partner (if there is an odd number, allow one trio with three-way play). Give each pair a copy of Workout Sheets #17 and #18 which you have cut apart and shuffled. Direct them to match significant elements of the passage by playing "concentration." Present these instructions: **Display your 16 cards upside down in four rows of four. Take turns turning over 2 cards. Confirm or disqualify the match by reading Philippians 2:1-11. One card from each pair includes the verse reference. If they match, keep them. If they don't, turn them back over. The person with the most matches wins.** Encourage pairs to spread out within the room so they have space to display their cards. Be certain that each pair has at least one Bible and that they understand that matches are made by completed verses, not by identical pictures.

When the game is over, humorously point out: **We kept score again! But even though only one of you technically won the game, both of you have won better understanding of Philippians 2:1-11.** Challenge: **Just**

as you concentrated to play the concentration game, concentrate on Jesus' way to make your family life happier. Ask for ways that the truth of the passage can promote good family relationships.

Emphasize that Jesus is exactly the one who can help us get rid of our feelings of jealousy, resentment, and anger. Rather than denying these feelings or being embarrassed about them, Jesus wants us to talk with Him about them.

OPTION

Instead of or in addition to the concentration game, write the lyrics to John Michael Talbot's "Philippians Canticle" with significant words left out. Give each student a copy and instruct them to fill in the blanks as they listen to the song. Because the song is Philippians 2:1-11 set to music, filling in the words highlights truths in the passage. Students will enjoy learning as they listen. You'll find the song on the album *Come to the Quiet* (Sparrow Records).

APPLYING THE TRUTH

AGREE/DISAGREE

Post these four signs on the four walls of your room:

AGREE	DISAGREE	STRONGLY AGREE	STRONGLY DISAGREE

To help your group clarify what humility means, direct them: **Come to the center of the room and stand in a huddle. When I make a statement, go to the sign that tells how you feel about the statement.** Read the first statement below. After students have moved to the feeling sign of their choice, encourage at least one person under each sign to explain his or her choice. Then supplement with the comments in parentheses. Repeat the process for the other statements.

- **Being humble means people will walk all over you.** (Sometimes they will, but often they see that you genuinely care, so they respond positively to you. Humility means you care about other's needs, not that you don't talk at all. Sometimes it meets a need to *not* let someone walk over you. Maybe it can teach them to care.)
- **Humility means giving up your rights.** (Yes, that's true. But it's also an active quality. As verses 3-4 explain, humility is forgetting your own needs, for a time, so you can meet the needs of others. In families these needs include understanding, attention, privileges, time. Usually humility motivates others to meet your needs too.)
- **Giving up your rights means you never tell other people when you are irritated with something they say or do.** (Not at all. There's nothing wrong with telling someone directly and lovingly that he or she is bothering you or neglecting you. That's part of learning how to live together as a family, and it creates the like-mindedness, love, and oneness of verse 2.)

- **Humility means being mousy, wishy-washy, spineless, and cowardly.** (Not at all. Jesus was quite gutsy and knew the right times to speak up and the right times to act. He gave up His rights precisely because He strongly believed His convictions about how to make people happy.)
- **If you deserve a position, you should demand it.** (Jesus didn't. People usually resent those who demand a position, a privilege, or a reward. Think about the friends and family members you respect the most. How do they handle their wisdom, their privileges, and their power?)
- **If you work to create oneness, tenderness, and compassion in your family, it will happen automatically.** (Not usually. Family oneness takes continual effort to achieve and maintain. And if your family members don't work with you, it's impossible to obtain. But your attitude might motivate other family members to work toward oneness too. IMPORTANT: You cannot control the actions of other family members; you don't have to feel guilty for what they do or don't do.)

JOURNAL MY PART

Say: **When we're thinking about our own rights and our frustrations about unfair treatment, we could forget that we might be taking away someone else's rights or that we might be treating someone unfairly. Let's journal our family interaction over the past 24–48 hours. If for some reason you haven't been home much, choose a day recently when you were.** Distribute paper and pencils. Then say: **Write down what you said or did to everyone in your family today (or yesterday).** (Sample beginning: I got up grouchy and snapped at my sister. She left me alone and then I cheered up some. I was pretty nice at breakfast since Dad made his famous pancakes. I said. . . .)

After students have completed their journal entries, have them label their completed writings as follows:
- Underline the put-downs.
- Circle the words that create closeness and like-mindedness.
- * Star attitudes like Jesus' attitudes.
- ⟡ Put an arrow next to attitudes that need to grow closer to Christlikeness.

Give each student another piece of paper and say: **Now on this paper, rewrite your journal as though you could live the day over again. Make your destructive conversations constructive and your good actions and attitudes even better.** If you have the student book, enlist two volunteers to dramatically read the conversation between Marie and her mother as an example of an honest but constructive parent/teen discussion.

Call for volunteers to read their actual interactions followed by their rewritten ones. Thank each who contributes. Point out: **Practicing talking with your family is as important as practicing for asking a girl out or practicing what you'd say on a date. When you have a difficult conversation or problem coming up, practice what you'll say, how you think your family member will respond, and what you could say next. Relationships are worth the time and work it takes to make them run smoothly.**

IMITATE CHRIST'S HUMILITY

Read Philippians 2:1-11 in circular fashion to conclude the session. Explain: **As we read I'd like all of you to stand with your Bibles open to Philippians 2:1-11. The person to my left reads until the first comma, then the next person reads until the next comma, and so on around the circle until we have read the entire passage.**

Close by leading a silent prayer focusing on students' specific unfair situations. Follow a pattern similar to this: **I'll now guide a time of silent prayer during which you can talk with God about your specific unfair situations. I'll suggest areas to focus on and then give you silent time to talk with God about them.** Pause to receive any questions and then continue: **Lord, it's not easy to be humble when we're treated unfairly. The situation in my home now that bothers me the most is** [about 20 seconds of silence]. **I think this situation happens because** [about 20 seconds of silence]. **It might help if I said** [about 20 seconds of silence]. **Or if I did** [about 20 seconds of silence]. **Lord, I don't always understand how humility and looking out for other's interests works, but I'm willing to try. I'll need Your help. One other thing I want to tell You is** [about 20 seconds of silence]. **Amen.**

CONCENTRATE ON • CHRIST

Encouragement from being united with Christ, comfort from His love, fellowship with the Spirit.

CONCENTRATE ON • CHRIST

"Ifs" from verse 1. Paul encouraged Christians to put these to use to create joy.

CONCENTRATE ON • CHRIST

Being like-minded, having the same love, being one in spirit and purpose.

CONCENTRATE ON • CHRIST

Three ways to make joy complete. Found in Philippians 2:2.

CONCENTRATE ON • CHRIST

Selfish ambition or vain conceit.

CONCENTRATE ON • CHRIST

Do nothing from (motivated by) these. Instead, consider others better than yourself (v. 3).

CONCENTRATE ON • CHRIST

Look not only to your own interests . . .

CONCENTRATE ON • CHRIST

. . . but also to the interests of others (v. 4).

CONCENTRATE
ON • CHRIST

Your attitude should be the same as . . .

CONCENTRATE
ON • CHRIST

. . . Jesus' attitude (v. 5).

CONCENTRATE
ON • CHRIST

Jesus had the nature of God . . .

CONCENTRATE
ON • CHRIST

. . . but instead of grasping equality with God He made Himself nothing and took on the nature of a servant (vv. 6–7).

CONCENTRATE
ON • CHRIST

Jesus was made in human likeness and showed His humility by . . .

CONCENTRATE
ON • CHRIST

. . . becoming obedient to death on the cross (v. 8).

CONCENTRATE
ON • CHRIST

God gave Jesus the highest place and the name that is above every name . . .

CONCENTRATE
ON • CHRIST

. . . that at the name of Jesus every knee shall bow and every tongue confess that He is Lord (vv. 9–11).

CONCENTRATE CONCENTRATE CONCENTRATE CONCENTRATE
ON • CHRIST ON • CHRIST ON • CHRIST ON • CHRIST

FAVORITISM, FIGHTS AND RIGHTS

SIBLING SKILLS (Genesis 27:1–28:9; 32:6-8; 33:1-11)

KEY CONCEPT

Age and need differences make it difficult for most siblings to get along. Seeing things from a sibling's perspective can help teens enjoy their families.

MEETING THE NEED

This session will respond to the following student questions and comments:
● "My brother gets into my stuff."
● "My mom favors my sister."
● "Why are big brothers and sisters so bossy?"

SESSION GOALS

You will help each group member
1. brainstorm ways siblings help and hinder their dreams for family happiness,
2. discover that sibling problems have occurred since early Bible days,
3. pinpoint some actions they can take to promote sibling closeness.

SPECIAL PREPARATION

____ Bring extra Bibles, pencils, paper, a chalkboard and chalk.
____ Bring the materials for "Custom-made Sibling."
____ Bring the student books if you have them.
____ Duplicate Workout Sheets #19 and #20.
____ Duplicate the Bible study assignments for "Nothing New."
____ Bring paper for the "Nothing New" drawings.
____ Prepare the "What Will I Do?" game.

BUILDING THE BODY

CUSTOM-MADE SIBLING

Provide clay, pipe cleaners, construction paper, scissors, markers, and tape at several stations. Direct teams of three to create the ideal sister or brother, labeling his or her qualities.

Call for the teams to present their creations. Tally the qualities they think make the ideal sibling. Note that answers may be direct like "understanding," and "sharing of ideas and experiences," or indirect like "stays out of my stuff" (meaning "gives me privacy") and "gives me a break" (meaning "accepts me unconditionally").

Discuss the experience with questions like: **What keeps siblings from being this way?** (Supplement with ideas from "The People You Love to Hate" in the student book and these samples: competition for parents' attention, differing personalities.) **How might we help our siblings develop the qualities we want?** (Supplement with "How Can We Get Along?" from the student book and these samples: be that way ourselves, say how we'd like them to be, pray that they'll listen to God's leadership.)

WORKOUT SHEET

Say: **Did you ever notice that *you* are a sibling? How do you think you measure up to this list of qualities?** Encourage students: **Though it's not the only factor, the way you act influences how your siblings act.** Distribute a copy of Workout Sheet #19 and give these instructions: **Write your name on this "report card" and grade yourself on your sibling qualities. (Don't sign the report card or fill in the comprehensive grade yet.) Then try to find a way to raise your grade at least one letter in at least one of these areas by the end of this session. I'll return them without reading them.** Ask them to fold their cards, write their names on the outside, and hand them to you.

WHAT CAN I DO?

Invite students to write problems they have with their sisters or brothers, explaining that you will collect them and read several at the end of the session (not revealing names) so the group can suggest solutions based on the truths they've discovered.

LAUNCHING THE LESSON

WISH LIST

Direct the group: **Close your eyes and dream about what you'd like your family to be like. . . . Now with your eyes still closed, call out**

one of your wishes. Write students' wishes on the chalkboard.

Instruct the group to open their eyes and look at the list. Ask: **How do sisters and brothers help or hinder our wishes? Choose one wish and tell one way siblings make this goal harder to achieve and one way a sibling could help you achieve it.**

Encourage your students: **We don't have to let problems with siblings overcome the pleasures! Focusing on the good things our siblings do can bring us joy and motivate us to work to get along with them.** Pause and then say: **Who would like to share something you like about your sister or brother?** (Share something about your own sibling.)

Acknowledge: **Some of you don't have or don't live with a sister or brother. But this session is still for you: you have friends with siblings; you may have cousins; and one day you may live with a roommate who will be like a sister or brother to you.**

EXPLORING THE WORD

NOTHING NEW

Tell this story without identifying its characters: **Once there were twin brothers with entirely different personalities. The mother favored the younger boy, who stayed inside. The father favored the more rustic, outdoorsy son. Their situation might have worked out just fine except the older son got more privileges. So the younger boy schemed to take these privileges from his older brother. To make matters even worse, the mother took the younger brother's side against her husband. Needless to say, the older twin felt like killing the younger. They spent over 20 years not speaking to each other before they were reunited.**

Ask: **When do you think this story took place?** Point out that this true story is recorded in Genesis, the first book of the Bible.

Divide the group into five teams and give each team one of the following assignments. Assure them that the content of the drawings is more important than the quality. Provide large paper and markers or crayons.

NOTE: You may be tempted to skip the drawing because of the time it takes. Before you do, consider these benefits: artistically minded youth will learn more by drawing than by discussing, and the posted drawings help the entire group understand the entire passage (because the story includes so many verses, the entire group cannot read it all).

Group 1
1. Read Genesis 27:1-17.
2. How did Rebekah show favoritism and encourage deception?
3. What do you think about Rebekah's encouraging Jacob to deceive his dad, even talking him out of worrying (v. 13) about doing wrong?
4. Draw a picture of the events in this passage, including the actions, emotions, and words you think are most important. Stick figures are fine, and you may include more than one scene. Let a different member of your team work on each scene.

Group 2

1. Read Genesis 27:18-29.
2. How did Jacob take advantage of his dad's blindness?
3. In what different ways did Jacob deceive his dad? (vv. 19, 20, 24, 27)
4. Draw a picture of the events in this passage, including the actions, emotions, and words you think are most important. Stick figures are fine, and you may include more than one scene. Let a different member of your team work on each scene.

Group 3

1. Read Genesis 27:30-41.
2. Esau and his dad were both angry. How did they show this? How did they show their sadness? Esau's anger and sadness turned to holding a _____ (v. 41).
3. Jacob's name means "deceiver" (v. 36). How did he live up to it?
4. Draw a picture of the events in this passage, including the actions, emotions, and words you think are most important. Stick figures are fine, and you may include more than one scene. Let a different member of your team work on each scene.

Group 4

1. Read Genesis 27:41–28:9.
2. Rebekah deceived her husband (v. 46). Why do you think she did this?
3. How does revenge play a part in this passage?
4. Draw a picture of the events in this passage, including the actions, emotions, and words you think are most important. Stick figures are fine, and you may include more than one scene. Let a different member of your team work on each scene.

Group 5

1. Read Genesis 32:6-8; 33:1-11.
2. After the two brothers were married and had several children, they got together after a long separation. How did Jacob feel about their meeting, and why do you think he felt this way?
3. Jacob had hurt Esau horribly. Why do you think Esau forgave him after so many years? (33:9-11)
4. Draw a picture of the events in this passage, including the actions, emotions, and words you think are most important. Stick figures are fine, and you may include more than one scene. Let a different member of your team work on each scene.

Call for each team to briefly describe the events it illustrated. Ask each team to explain how the parents and sons contributed to the problem, and to suggest how it could have been avoided.

LEARNING FROM THEIR MISTAKES

Write this sentence-starter on the chalkboard: **I am like Jacob/Esau when _____, but because I know the results of that action/ attitude, I'll....** Direct each student to complete the sentence by filling in the blank, choosing from the options, and adding an ending. Examples:
● I'm like Jacob when I take advantage of my sister, but because I know the results of that action, I will work for her best as well as mine.

● I'm like Esau when I want to kill my brother, but because I know the results of that attitude, I'll talk with God and with my brother about my anger until I can forgive him and decide what to do next.

APPLYING THE TRUTH

BOTH SIDES NOW

Point out that seeing problems from a sister's or brother's point of view helps siblings avoid the selfish and hurtful behavior that Jacob and Esau fell into. Help students find partners who match their home situations as closely as possible. For example, a younger brother of an older sister should find someone who is an older sister of a younger brother.

Distribute Workout Sheet #20 and instruct pairs: **Choose at least one of these situations and rewrite it from the point of view of the sister or brother. Help your partner to understand the point of view you play at home.** If you have student books, point out the samples in chapter 10. OPTION: Students may want to rewrite a situation of their own instead.

Call for volunteers to read their rewrites, and affirm the value of looking at problems from the other person's point of view.

WHAT I WILL DO?

Prepare the human board game "What Will I Do?" by these steps:
A. Pieces of construction paper will become your game spaces and students themselves will be the markers. Determine how many game spaces you need based on the size of your room and how many turns you want each student to have before reaching the end of the "board." On a third of the space pieces write "What?"; on a third of the spaces write "Why?"; on a third of the spaces write "How?" Shuffle these and lay them on the floor to form a winding road. (OPTION: If space is limited, modify any board game by taping "How?" "Why?" or "What?" on the spaces. Use the game's markers.)
B. Bring a spinner borrowed from a board game. (If you can't find one make a stack of cards marked *1, 2,* or *3.* Players draw a card to move.)
C. Cut apart a copy of Workout Sheet #20 and place it in an envelope. If you did "What Can I Do?" earlier, add those problems.
D. Write the rules on the chalkboard.

Play the game according to the following rules and using questions like the ones suggested here.

Game Rules
1. Spin the spinner (or draw a card) to tell how many spaces to move.
2. When a player lands on a "What?" space, the leader asks "what" the Bible says.
3. For a "Why?" space, the leader asks "why" the player thinks something is true.
4. For a "How?" space, the leader asks for a suggestion on "how" to solve a certain situation.

5. If a player answers correctly, he may spin (or draw) in his next turn. If he does not answer correctly, he does not move on his next turn, but must answer another question from the same category.
6. Players should keep their Bibles opened to Genesis 27–28, 32–33.

Suggested Questions (Those marked + can be used more than once.)

What?
   1. What person in Genesis 27 encouraged her son to deceive his father? (Rebekah)
   2. What brothers in Genesis 27 who had trouble getting along? (Jacob and Esau)
 +3. What feeling(s) did Jacob have about meeting Esau after so many years? (Any of these is correct: Fear; distress; like defending himself; like crying; gratefulness for finding favor.)
 +4. In what way(s) did Jacob take advantage of his dad's blindness? (Any of these is correct: Said he was Esau; covered himself with fur to feel like Esau; wore Esau's clothes to smell like Esau.)
   5. What does Jacob's name mean? (Deceiver, 27:36.)
 +6. In what ways did Esau and his father show their anger and sadness over Jacob taking the blessing? (Any of these: Isaac trembled violently; Esau cried loudly and bitterly; Esau remembered the meaning of Jacob's name; Isaac said, "What can I do for you, my son?"; Esau wept aloud.)
   7. Why do you think Jacob and Esau waited so long to reunite? (Opinion) What do you think motivated them then? (Opinion)

Why?
 +1. Why does it seem easier to find fault than to compliment?
 +2. Why do you think holding a grudge is easier than forgiving?
 +3. Why do you think forgiveness works?
 +4. Why is it hard to admit you are wrong?
 +5. Why do you think understanding works better than keeping score?
 +6. Why do you think most brothers and sisters fight?
 +7. Why is it hard to be fair in families?
 +8. Why do you think parents play favorites?
 +9. Why does admitting you are wrong promote closeness?
 +10. Why is it hard to get along with the people we live with?

How?
Draw a situation from the problem envelope (created from Workout Sheet #20 and "What Can I Do?") and ask "How might you work with your sibling (rather than against her) to solve this situation?"

HOW'S MY GRADE?

Give the students their copies of Workout Sheet #19 and have them re-grade themselves on each of the sibling skills as they now understand and plan to use them. When they have finished, call for volunteers to share an area in which they feel they can make a better grade and how they would do it. (Example: Give my little sister attention by playing her favorite board game with her.) Direct students to sign their report cards.

REPORT CARD

A	B	C	D	F
excellent	good	average	needs lots of improvement	totally self-centered

R E P O R T C A R D

1 ____ I try to understand my brother's/sister's personality and interests.

2 ____ I consider the needs of my sibling, as well as my own needs.

3 ____ I give my sibling attention at least sometime during the day.

4 ____ I listen to my sibling both when s/he's sad and when s/he's happy.

5 ____ I see my sibling as a person, not a problem.

6 ____ When problems arise, I work with, rather than against, my sibling.

7 ____ I treat my sibling as Jesus would.

8 ____ I refuse to let my bad moods cause me to torment my sibling.

9 ____ I try to be happy when my sibling gets attention from my parents, knowing that my turn is coming.

10 ____ I use my power constructively rather than destructively.

_____ MY COMPREHENSIVE GRADE ON SIBLING SKILLS

Because my relationship with my sibling will last throughout life, I will try to keep it growing closer and closer.

Signed,

_____

SIDES TO THE STORY

Choose one of these situations and write it from the point of view of the sister or brother causing the problem.

Whenever a friend comes over, my younger brother hangs around and bothers us. I know there aren't many boys his age in the neighborhood, but I wish he'd give me privacy at least part of the time!

I do something and get in trouble for it and then the next day my little sister does the same thing and doesn't get in trouble. And it's not one of those things where I know better and she doesn't.

Any time my friends are around, my sister embarrasses me by saying or doing dumb things. In fact, when Greg came to pick me up last night, she said, "She's been getting ready for you for two hours. You must really be something!"

My big brother is different from me and expects me to be like him. Because I'd rather read than play sports, he calls me a sissy or a wimp.

My sister really knows how to frustrate me. She bugs me until I can't stand her anymore and I do something mean to her. Then *I* get in trouble for something she egged on.

Dad and Mom play favorites. My sister is real smart in school and they're always asking me why I can't be as smart as she is. My grades are average but my soccer skills are superior. Why can't I get recognition for that? There is more than one way to be smart!

FAVORITISM, FIGHTS, AND RIGHTS

THEY'RE DRIVING ME CRAZY! (Selected Psalms)

KEY CONCEPT

Loving understanding and clear communication can minimize persistent family irritations.

MEETING THE NEED

This session will respond to the following student comments:
- "My parents won't even talk about our disagreements."
- "My parents are too strict."
- "My sister embarrasses me by wanting to go places with me."

SESSION GOALS

You will help each group member
1. evaluate and respond to family irritations,
2. express his or her feelings to God about family relationships,
3. identify extended family members who can help meet relationship needs.

SPECIAL PREPARATION

____ Bring extra Bibles, pencils, paper, construction paper, and markers.
____ Prepare relays for "Stacked Against Me."
____ Bring the student books if you have them.
____ If you have no student books, write the five questions for "We're All in This Together" on the board.
____ Duplicate Workout Sheets #21 and #22.

BUILDING THE BODY

STACKED AGAINST ME

Play several relays in which some teams have unfair advantages or handicaps. Examples: In tic-tac-toe, one team always gets to go first; in relays, one team always plays with two fewer players; in board games, one starts with more play money. Possible relays: Balloon between the knees; paper plate on the head; run to one wall, put on oversized shirt and pants, run to second wall and take them off, run back to origin. Ignore complaints of unfairness and insist that teams do their best in what they have.

Follow up the games by acknowledging that some teams started with handicaps. Then say: **Real life is like that. Sometimes, through no fault of our own, we're in homes where things really are unfair, where our parents' attitudes or personal problems make day-to-day life extremely difficult. The parents might be too strict, or unloving, or abusive, or unavailable. What advice would you give to a teenager in this situation?** Supplement with comments like: Pray for strength; make the best of it; get outside help; realize you can help make your own family better; know it's not your fault; spend time with happy families to learn better ways to love.

LAUNCHING THE LESSON

WE'RE ALL IN THIS TOGETHER

Give each student two slips of paper and a pencil. Give these instructions: **On one of the pieces of paper write something your parents do (or don't do) that drives you crazy. It can be a habit, a rule, an expression, a character trait, or whatever you want it to be. And it can be a family member besides your parent. Do not sign your paper. Place it in my envelope.** Gather the papers as students finish.

When all have finished, say: **Now on the second paper write something you do or say that irritates your parents, or siblings, or other family members.** Collect them and read one at a time, asking: **How do parents tell teenagers they don't like this irritating action?** (Examples: Yell; tell me to stop; explain what irritates them and why.) When all actions have been read and responded to, ask: **How do you like your parents to let you know you're irritating them?** (Answers will vary but probably be something like: Tell me calmly; ask rather than tell me to stop.)

Say: **I encourage you to use the same irritation-fighting techniques with your parents that you like them to use with you. I'd like to suggest five questions that can guide you toward solving family irritations.** Point out these five questions in their student books (or on a poster or chalkboard):
1. Why is this action or attitude so irritating?
2. Why does my parent (or other family member) do this?

3. What might I have done to contribute to the problem?
4. What could I say or do to encourage my parent to stop it or to do something different?
5. If it's not realistic to expect the parent to change, or if the parent doesn't change, what could I do to get used to the irritation or to understand it better?

Shuffle and redistribute the papers on which students wrote family irritations so that no one has his or her own paper. Have each student write answers to the five questions above, including advice he or she thinks God would suggest for solving the problem. Chapter 11 of the student book offers two examples.

After several minutes, call on volunteers to read their problems and advice. Encourage the other students to add ideas. Read as many problems as your introductory time allows. If you do not have the student books, encourage students to copy the five questions to take home.

Make a transition into the Bible study by explaining: **Talking about family frustrations arouses many feelings. God knows that and understands. Let's read some psalms that express feelings we may be experiencing.**

EXPLORING THE WORD

DOODLE SHEET

Call for three volunteers to read these psalms with as much emotion as possible: Psalm 55; Psalm 56; Psalm 64. Encourage your students to doodle about the emotions expressed as they listen. Provide scrap paper and pencils.

Ask: **What feelings did you doodle?** (Examples: Sadness; despair; hopelessness turned to hope; confidence; security; happiness.) **Are our parents our enemies?** (No, but sometimes we feel like they are; telling these feelings to God helps us know what to do about them.)

Call for a fourth volunteer to read Psalm 32. Ask: **How is this psalm different from the other three?** (The writer realizes he has done something wrong and confesses to free himself from the weight of guilt.) Recall the exercise above when students wrote ways they irritated others in their families. Ask: **When might we be at fault in family frustrations?** (Examples: Might have egged it on; might have been insensitive to a mood and forced our parents to blow up.) **How might unconfessed sin add to our sadness?** (Examples: We might realize we did wrong but not want to admit it; would feel guilty; guilt feelings keep us from talking honestly about the problem.)

Call for a fifth volunteer to read Psalm 46:1-7. Ask: **How is this psalm different?** (Example: It's a psalm of confidence in a time of trouble.) **When might you want to read it?** (Examples: When you had already complained to God and had discovered what to do, and you wanted to thank God for His power and wisdom; to thank God for getting you through a problem.)

Ask: **Which of these three types of psalms would you most like to read when you're frustrated about family events?** (Opinions will vary; may want to read different ones at different times, depending on the type of event or frustration.)

WORKOUT SHEET

Distribute Workout Sheet #21 and tell students to write their own psalms to God about family situations that make them feel sad and frustrated. Suggest they use one of the psalms they have just read as a model. Be sure everyone has a Bible. Assure them that they don't have to use every verse in the psalm they choose. Circulate and encourage.

After several minutes, call for volunteers to read their psalms. Compliment each. Suggest that psalm-writing is a type of prayer to God, and that God wants to hear their sad as well as happy feelings. He has the answers for both.

CARE ENOUGH TO SEND THE BEST

Hand out construction paper, markers, pencils, and pens. Direct students: **Create a greeting card you could send to someone with family frustrations. Let your card suggest a Bible promise that would remind your friend of God's love and could help him or her know just what to do. This promise could be from one of the psalms we just studied or another promise you yourself depend on.**

Encourage volunteers to show and explain their greeting cards. Say something positive about each. Suggest: **Send the card if you like. Or keep it in your own room as a reminder of God's ever-present care and always effective power.** Point out: **Even when God doesn't change the situation, He equips us to handle it. And He heals us to keep us from repeating the same mistakes in our friendships and future families.**

APPLYING THE TRUTH

WORKOUT SHEET

Ask: **What is a pet peeve?** (Persistent complaint, gripe, or grievance.) Give each student a copy of Workout Sheet #22 and explain: **These are gripes teens have listed about their parents.** Guide groups of three to: **Choose at least two actions or attitudes that might heal the source of each pet peeve. Feel free to add actions and attitudes not on this Workout Sheet. Then write at least one of your own pet peeves at the bottom and select or write in healing actions and attitudes.**

When groups have finished, and before reporting suggested attitudes or actions that could help with each pet peeve, ask: **Which of these pet**

peeves is the worst to live with and why? Then ask for solutions to each pet peeve, encouraging students to tell why it would work and to give an example of how to do it. Allow plenty of time for discussion.

NOT ALL ENDINGS ARE HAPPY

Say: **Even when we try all these actions, things still might not be as good as we'd like them to be. That's because our parents and other family members have to work with us. Most will, but not all will. When we become frustrated by our home situations, we feel like just getting out. We think if we can just leave, things will be better. But it's not that easy. Your relationship with your parents, good or bad, lasts a lifetime.** To illustrate, read this letter from an adult about her parents:

Even though I'm married and have my own children, I still care about what my mother and father think. The bad part is that they don't care about me. Oh, they pretend they do—they have the holiday get-togethers and send birthday cards and all those obvious family things. But there's no joy in it. And when it comes down to the things that matter, they don't (or can't) care. If I express a worry, they call me foolish. If I voice a dream, they tell me it's no use trying. When I accomplish something, they take no notice. When I need them, they say I'm calling at an inconvenient time. I know that it's their problem, that because they aren't happy themselves they can't reach out to someone else, but it still hurts. I know I shouldn't worry about it, that it's not my fault, but I worry anyway. The thing that helps the most is to quit investing in them. I just set myself up for disappointment when I do. So I share my excitement with my husband and friends and simply treat my parents as though they are acquaintances. Relationships have to go two ways—and all I can do is my way. The best part is that God has helped me overcome the hurt to learn to love my present family. It hasn't been easy, but overall I've learned what's important in families.

Ask: **Why does this person hurt so much? Why can't she just leave her parents behind? Why does a parent's opinion matter so much? What else can she do to make her parents' attitude easier to take? How is her situation like yours? What other examples can you give of an unhappy ending?** (Examples: Never curing alcoholism; parent dying before problem worked out.)

Why should we keep on loving, or trying to love, even when it's hard? (God calls us to; we continue to grow.) **When is it best to withdraw?** (Hard to tell, but usually when our parents keep discouraging us or we stay depressed; talk to an adult to help decide.)

Assure teens that, though their relationships with their parents may never be what they want them to be, they can create happy relationships with their own future spouses and children. And, unlike human fathers and mothers, God, the Heavenly Father, will not disappoint us (Romans 9:33). His perfect love can heal the family pain we experience. He can turn unhappy endings into happy futures.

RELATIVELY HAPPY

Distribute paper and markers and say: **Sometimes a relative can meet your needs in a way a parent can't or won't. Draw a picture of your extended family and what you like about each member.** Explain that extended family includes aunts, uncles, cousins, grandparents, stepparents, and other relatives who may or may not live in the same house.

As students display their drawings, discuss them with such questions as: **How might you grow even closer to the aunt, uncle, or grandparent you like?** (Examples: Phone calls; visits; cards; cassette tapes on which you send messages.) **Why is it sometimes easier to feel close to an extended family member? Share something you especially like about one or more of your extended family members.**

THE BEST WE CAN DO

Close with sentence prayer. Give these instructions: **We'll go around the circle twice. Each of you say a phrase or sentence to God about your family situation. You might want to ask for help in dealing with a frustration, thank God for something good, praise Him for a relative you like, or ask for strength to do what God has already asked you to do.** If you have several visitors or want to give the option, allow students to silently squeeze the hand next to them if they choose not to pray aloud.

Read Jeremiah 29:11 as an encouragement of God's good plans for our present and future.

WRITE YOUR OWN

PSALM

"Psalm" very simply means "song." What do you want to sing to God about your family? Include both your frustrations and ways you've solved (or would like to solve) them. Choose one of these psalms and change the words to say what you want to say: Psalm 32; 46:1–7; 55; 56; 64. Notice that the psalmist started out discouraged, but talking with God gave him strength and the ability to handle his problems.

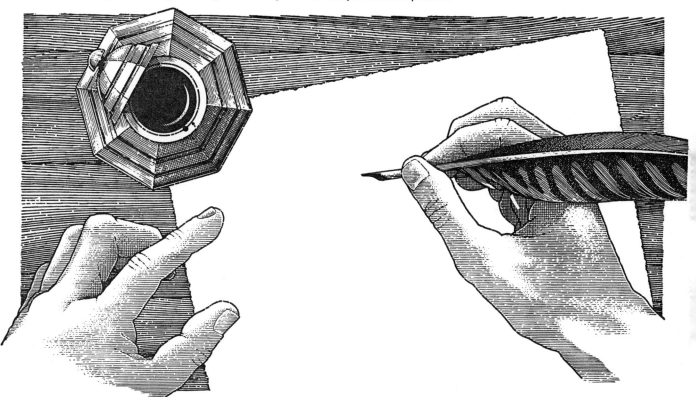

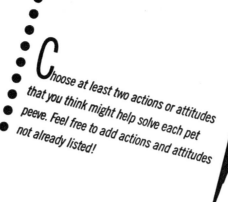

Choose at least two actions or attitudes that you think might help solve each pet peeve. Feel free to add actions and attitudes not already listed!

PET PEEVES

—— My parents are too strict. It's not that I'm being selfish—they really are unfair.

—— We have to go to all this family stuff and it's boring. Hardly any of the cousins are my age and the adults just sit around and talk.

—— My parents won't talk about our disagreements. It's their way or no way at all. They don't even listen to my side of the story.

—— My parents lecture rather than listen.

—— My mom stays on me about keeping my room clean.

—— My dad's temper is unbearable. He flies off the handle at the least little thing and then everything is tense.

—— My parent doesn't seem to realize that I'm old enough to make my own decisions.

—— My dad embarrasses me by wanting to go places with me.

PET PEEVE SOLUTIONS

1 Complain to God about it.

2 Search for the reason they act/think that way.

3 Be as cooperative as possible.

4 Show that I can be trusted for extra privileges by keeping current rules, curfews, doing chores, etc.

5 Find an adult who will listen and help me think through and decide what to do about my problem. (Maybe a grandparent, an aunt, a worker at my church.)

6 Talk with a friend in a similar situation.

7 Keep my own emotions calm.

8 Remember that parents are people like I am.

9 Read 1 Corinthians 13:4–7 and Galatians 5:22–23 for action ideas.

10 Endure the situation until I'm on my own or in college.

11 Demonstrate respect by _____.

12 Read Psalms or Proverbs.

13 _____

FAVORITISM, FIGHTS, AND RIGHTS

I'D NEVER DO THAT TO MY KIDS! (Selected passages)

KEY CONCEPT

With God's help, teens can take deliberate steps to keep from repeating their parents' mistakes.

MEETING THE NEED

This session will respond to the following student comments:
- "I won't do that in my family!"
- "I'll understand my kids when I'm a parent."
- "My parents don't remember what it's like to be young."

SESSION GOALS

You will help each group member
1. identify characteristics that he wants in his future family if he becomes a parent,
2. reword destructive phrases to obey Ephesians 6:4,
3. write himself a letter of advice about family life.

SPECIAL PREPARATION

____ Bring pencils, paper, 3" x 5" cards, and markers.
____ Bring magazines and other materials for "Picture Perfect."
____ Bring a light bulb for each student and glass-marking pens.
____ Write the topics for "60-Second Speeches."
____ Duplicate the WANTED assignments and Workout Sheets.
____ Bring the student books if you have them.
____ Tape-record the messages for "A Better Way to Say It."

BUILDING THE BODY

PICTURE PERFECT

As students enter, direct them to one of the corners where you've placed a piece of poster board, magazines with many pictures and advertisements, scissors, and glue. Post these instructions at each corner: **Create a group collage of pictures and words that describe a happy family. Cut them from the magazines or draw them yourself.** Encourage the early arrivers to get started and the later arrivers to join the groups already in progress.

After several minutes, call for each group to display and describe their collage. Then ask each group member: **Tell one way your present family is like this collage and one way it is different.** About halfway through the sharing, tell a similarity and difference for the family in which you grew up.

Point out: **The first step to creating your own happy family if you get married, or a happy relationship with roommates if you stay single, is to notice what you want to repeat and what you want to change about the family you currently live in. You have each stated at least one way you want to repeat your family happiness and one way you want to improve it. If we don't take conscious steps to change, we'll repeat almost everything we grew up with. Let's learn how God can help us create family happiness both now and in our own future families.**

I SEE THE LIGHT!

Call on a volunteer to read 1 John 1:5-7. Ask: **What does this have to do with family life?** (Examples: God is like light to guide us when our family situations seem dark; when we know God's ways to live happily in families, we should live by them.)

Give each student a light bulb. Direct them: **Go to the table and draw or write on your light bulb bits of light you've seen during the past several weeks of study on surviving at home (and enjoying it). On the table are permanent glass markers.** When they have finished ask: **Who would like to share one truth you've learned during our family study?** Encourage several to say a sentence or two. Suggest they take their light bulbs home and use them in a lamp in their room as a constant reminder of God's light.

LAUNCHING THE LESSON

60-SECOND SPEECHES

Write these actions on slips of paper and place them in an envelope: LOYALTY, UNDERSTANDING, FORGIVENESS, HONESTY, RESPECT,

CONFESSION OF WRONG, PAMPERING, COMPLIMENTING, LISTENING, CRITICISM, GOSSIP, BACKBITING, BETRAYAL, POUTING, DEMANDING, CONTROLLING. Each student will draw an action from the envelope and make a 60-second speech on how the action can make or break family happiness. If someone doesn't like the action he drew, he may draw again and choose between the two. Point out: **Notice that some of these actions can be good or bad, depending on how they are used. You might want to talk about both sides in your speech.** Let volunteers go first. Continue taking turns until everyone has spoken.

After each speech, reinforce a significant comment and thank that speaker for his or her insight. After all the speeches say: **You notice that there were more positives than negatives. That's where we'd like to focus today: positive actions we can take to create happy families.**

> ### WANTED: HAPPY FAMILY LIFE

Duplicate each of the following WANTED assignments. Divide the group into pairs, and suggest these directions: **I have five elements of family life that affect all of us in some way. Choose one and write a want ad detailing actions that will qualify someone for this position. The questions with each will help guide your thinking.**
- **WANTED: someone who will talk instead of yell.** Because yelling is often a symptom of fear, anger, frustration, or worry, how might this person express those emotions without yelling?
- **WANTED: someone who can give advice without pushing.** What are the best ways to give advice? How should this person give advice like/differently from your parents?
- **WANTED: someone who won't get upset when I tell about a problem.** What people make you comfortable talking about problems? How do people show they accept you?
- **WANTED: a parent who will trust me and whom I can trust.** How will this person show he believes in you? How will he show that you can trust him? How will you encourage each other to be trustworthy?
- **WANTED: family member who is not a parent.** What do your grandparents, aunts, and uncles do for you that you like? How might they be even better? What would you like them to do that they don't do? How might you grow to be a good relative?

Call for students to read their want ads. Point out: **The things you wrote in these ads are tips for developing close family qualities in yourself. What were some of these?** (Examples: Understand; say feelings directly; listen rather than lecture.)

EXPLORING THE WORD

> ### WORKOUT SHEET

Point out: **The Bible encourages us to become good family members. To discover how, unscramble the verses on this Workout Sheet and**

match them to the verse references written at the top of the Workout Sheet. Reading each verse will help you unscramble them. Give each student a copy of Workout Sheet #23 and encourage them to work in pairs. Notice that as they unscramble the verses, students repeatedly read the Bible promises. This helps settle them in their minds.

Call for students to read the unscrambled verses one at a time and to identify their Bible location. (Answers: 1 John 1:5b; Ephesians 5:8-10; Ephesians 5:15-16; Ephesians 6:4; James 1:19; James 1:22.) Ask: **What does it mean to walk in the light?** (Examples: Love as Jesus loves; live by God's truth as taught in the Bible.) **Who can give an example of this in family life?** (Examples: Love each other as we love ourselves; be patient even when we're feeling grouchy.) **Why do we sometimes ignore God's light?** (Examples: We don't stop to think about Him; we may mistakenly think He doesn't care about our family lives.) **How might we remind ourselves to live by God's light?** (Examples: Try it; ask God for power to do so.)

A BETTER WAY TO SAY IT

Call on a volunteer to read Ephesians 6:4. Ask: **What does exasperate mean?** (To make angry; annoy; irritate.)

Play a tape on which you have recorded the following messages (*without* the comments in parentheses). Leave a space between the messages to allow for turning the tape on and off. Say: **These recorded messages demonstrate ways a parent might exasperate his children. I'd like you to reword the same messages in ways that obey Ephesians 6:4—"to bring them up in the training and instruction of the Lord."** Call on a different volunteer to play and reword each message. After each volunteer has played a message, ask: **Why might a parent exasperate his children this way?** Invite others to add ideas about the same message. Then supplement with the comments in parentheses.

- **You'll never amount to anything if you keep getting grades like this!** (Dad might say this because he's worried; could be restated: "I imagine you're just as disappointed as I am about these grades. What do you think would help you pull them up?")
- **You never do anything around this house! What do you think I am, your maid?** (Mother is probably tired after a long day and feels the burden of housekeeping is on her shoulders. Could be restated, "I'm really tired and I need your help. Could you pick up while I vacuum?")
- **I thought you were smarter than that.** (Parent is sad that teenager has made a poor choice and is suffering for it. Could be restated, "I'm sad that this has happened to you. I hate to see you hurt like this.")
- **Do it because I said so!** (Parent is convinced she is right because of experience. Could be restated, "These are the reasons I think this is best. . . .")
- **I can't believe you said that!** (Parent is worried that the teenager will do or say the bad thing she has talked about. Could be restated, "Why do you think God forbids that?" or "What do you think would happen if you tried it?")
- **I've been worried about you, so I read the notes in your top drawer.** (Parent is worried and tries to get inside story. Could be restated, "You haven't been yourself lately, and I'm so worried that I'm tempted to read your notes to find out why. Will you fill me in?")

Ask: **What might children do to make it easy for parents to exasperate them?** (Examples: Be grouchy; not tell them anything.) **What might you do to make your parents respond positively to you?** (Examples: Listen to parents as you want them to listen to you; talk honestly but caringly.) **How might you respond if your parent does exasperate you?** (Examples: Avoid reacting in same way parent is acting; calm down before reacting.)

Lead the group in a discussion of how teenagers exasperate parents (and other family members). Use questions like:
- **How can we keep from being exasperating?** (Examples: Catch ourselves before we speak; restate what we're feeling; think about how our parents will feel about what we say.)
- **Why is it better to change our words before they come out of our mouths?** (Examples: Can't take the words back; they might hurt or discourage someone.)
- **Does a true Christian ever say or do something that hurts another?** (Yes, we all make mistakes.)
- **What should we do then?** (Examples: Apologize; rethink and change the wording to say what we really want to say; request forgiveness; try not to repeat the offense.)
- **How can we learn to act and speak lovingly to family members?** (Examples: Practice doing so; be sensitive to which actions and words are hurtful.)

Read James 1:22 as an encouragement to put love into practice.

APPLYING THE TRUTH

WORKOUT SHEET

Distribute copies of Workout Sheet #24. Instruct students: **Write yourself a letter about things you want to do and don't want to do if you have teenage children someday. The sentence-starters on the Workout Sheet are suggestions only. Feel free to add your own better ideas.**

If you have the student books, point out examples under "Practice What You Preach." Invite volunteers to read their completed sentences. Encourage your students to keep their letters to reread if and when they become parents.

Explain: **We must take deliberate steps to change our parents' negative patterns. If not, we tend to repeat what we were brought up with. Why?** (Because we unconsciously imitate the way we were brought up.)

If you have the student book, read the four steps under "The Position is Filled" as examples of deliberate action. Ask: **How else might we change patterns?**

Summarize: **I am quite proud of your eagerness to do things right. Your parents do many things right with you and I pray you'll do even better. With God's help you can create a marriage and a home that will bring temendous happiness. I encourage you to do so if marriage is part of His plan for you!**

YOU CAN DO IT!

To close, and to allow students to encourage one another, give each a 3″ x 5″ card and instruct them: **Write your name vertically on this card. Pass it to the right. You who now hold the cards, write one way that person can create family happiness in her present home or future home, starting with one letter of her name. For example, you might use the "C" in "Nicole" to say "Calm down before you talk about an explosive issue." All suggestions must be positive and realistic. You wouldn't want to say, "Just stay in your room to keep from fighting." That might keep things quieter but it wouldn't make things happier!**

Allow time to write a suggestion and help any who struggle. Then instruct them: **Now pass the cards again and use another letter of the name in your hand.** After they've had time to write a suggestion, pass the cards again. Say: **If all letters are used by the time a name gets to you, use a letter a second time.** Repeat the passing and suggestion procedure about five times.

Instruct students: **Now return the cards to their owners by passing them back the way they came. Would any of you like to tell about a suggestion you received and how you plan to implement it?** Allow at least 10 seconds of silence to encourage students to speak. After all who have wanted to speak have spoken (and it's OK if not many do), say, **You may have heard a suggestion that is not on your card but that you'd like to try. Write it on your card now.** After a moment of writing, suggest: **Keep your card in your top drawer or another place you'll see it often.**

CAUSE FOR CONFIDENCE

Read Philippians 1:6 as a promise of confidence that God will work in your group's present and future family skills. Point out that only in God's strength can we create the happy families we want and need.

SORT IT OUT

Unscramble these verses for some good advice on getting along with your family. Then write the verse reference in the blank. The verses: James 1:19; Ephesians 5:8–10; Ephesians 5:15–16; Ephesians 6:4; James 1:22; 1 John 1:5b (from the *New International Version*).

_____

at is is in no darkness light; there all. Him God

_____

consists of all for and For you you were once light light light darkness, children righteousness but now are in in the the the Lord. Live as fruit of goodness, truth.

_____

Do Do not listen to the word, and yourselves. so what it says. merely deceive

_____

because Be but very careful, then, days how evil. you live—not as are as wise, unwise making the the most of every opportunity,

_____

My man's dear desires. bring brothers, become take to to to this: Everyone should be listen, slow quick angry, anger speak and slow for does not about the righteous life that God note of

_____

and in of do them not exasperate your Fathers, instead, bring up the instruction training the children; Lord.

I'll Never Do That To My Kids!

I hereby pledge that if I am ever a parent:

I will never...

I will always...

When my kids want to talk to me about
a problem I'll...

I will let my kids...

To encourage my kids to make their own
smart choices, I'll...

I especially want to remember to...

FAMILY SURVIVAL GUIDE
EVALUATION SHEET

Dear Leader,
You can have a real impact on future Young Teen Feedback Electives! Please take a minute to fill out this form giving us your candid reaction to this material. Thanks for your help.

ABOUT YOU
In what setting did you use this elective? (Sunday School, youth group, midweek Bible study, etc.)
_____

How many young people were in your group? _____

What was the age-range of those in your group? _____

How many weeks did you spend on this study? _____

How long was your average meeting time? _____

(Optional)   Name _____

Address _____

ABOUT THIS YOUNG TEEN FEEDBACK ELECTIVE
Did you and your young people enjoy this study? (Why or why not?)

What are the strengths and weaknesses of this leader's book?

Did you use the student books?   _____ Yes   _____ No
   If so, what are their strengths and weaknesses?

ABOUT THE FUTURE
What topics and issues would you like to see covered in future electives?

What Bible studies would you like to see included in future electives?

Do you plan to use other Young Teen Feedback Electives? (Why or why not?)

Do you plan to repeat this study in the future with new students? (Why or why not?)

SonPower Youth Sources Editor
1825 College Avenue
Wheaton, Illinois 60187